W9-DCC-550

The Christian as Communicator

Westminster Studies in Christian Communication

Kendig Brubaker Cully, General Editor

The Christian as Communicator

HARRY A. DEWIRE

THE WESTMINSTER PRESS
Philadelphia

LIBRARY OF CONGRESS CATALOG CARD NO. 60-14681

PRINTED IN THE UNITED STATES OF AMERICA

To

Marian

Contents

Editor's Note 9

Preface 11

I. Communication and Christian Responsibility 13

II. Christians Are Persons 37

III. "If I Speak in the Tongues of Men . . ." 63

IV. ". . . And Have Not Love" 90

V. Christian Talks to Christian 113

VI. The Gesture Toward the "Other" 141

VII. Authority in the Raised Question 166

Notes 187

Bibliography 191

Index 195

A Note on Westminster Studies in Christian Communication

These Studies, for which the first two volumes are foundational, are predicated on the ground that the Christian faith needs to be made relevant to persons in the modern world in terms of the dynamic nature of the faith itself and the channels that are capable of conveying such a faith. In itself any technique of communication conceivably could serve as well for secular as for religious ends. In this series a wide variety of means and methods of communication will be analyzed in the light of their availability to, and suitability for, the particular tasks that the Christian church faces in bringing the realities of faith to bear upon the life of actual persons in the contemporary situation.

Oftentimes in the past, techniques have been viewed almost as ends in themselves. Or, they have been taken over uncritically from the secular culture without being subjected to adequate scrutiny as to whether they are appropriate for the church's use. On the other hand, sometimes the church has been blind to the life situations of the present to such an extent as to ignore the real ways in which people's lives are influenced by all that impinges on them. In the latter case, the church has failed to bring the life-giving power of the gospel to bear on contemporary culture because of a lack of understanding of, or appreciation for, the means of communication that have been proved capable of changing lives and societies.

Involving as it does both the "What" and the "How," the whole question of the communication of the gospel in the modern world is pivotal in the present juncture of history. Starting with these initial volumes, the present Studies will be aimed at bringing the "What" and the "How" together fruitfully.

These books are designed to make a contribution to the ongoing conversations across boundaries. Theology, Biblical studies, sociology, cultural anthropology, psychology, education, art, letters, science, and the other disciplines, all have something to say to one another. In our present concern, "communication" refers to the way in which the Christian faith can come into conjunction with what is happening in the total world of life and ideas in the middle decades of the twentieth century. In each of these Studies attention will focus on some important aspect of the basic question: How can the church most effectively preach, teach, and otherwise manifest the gospel in the growing edges of man's present-day culture? No aspect of man's actual situation is alien to such a question. No medium of communication should fail to come under scrutiny if, as Christians, we are eager to have the Word of God confront a confused generation powerfully and compellingly.

Each volume in Westminster Studies in Christian Communication will be an authentic voice of one perceptive interpreter. No effort has been made to suggest to any writer what "line" he ought to follow. Each work will be adjudged by the readers on its own merits. The writers themselves conceivably might disagree heartily with regard to certain presuppositions or conclusions held by their colleagues. All this will be to the good if the result of these Studies should be the stimulating of many conversations. Yet all the writers have in mind a focus that is realistic, an emphasis that is practical, and a discussion that is timely. The only request made of the authors is that they speak out of their knowledge to the very heart and mind of our times. Depth without dullness, breadth without diffuseness, challenge without sentimentality — these, at least, it is hoped, will be characteristic of all the Studies. We are grateful to those who have consented to share in this venture into communication, and we commend their work as in itself an integral part of the church's task of communication.

KENDIG BRUBAKER CULLY

Evanston, Illinois *General Editor*

Preface

Sound has always been powerful, more powerful than logic or sense. It attracts us, and is especially impressive when it assumes word form. But sound, even word sounds uttered in uncounted billions on behalf of mankind, has not prevented us from persisting in the illogical behavior of war or the nonsensical attitude of prejudice.

The failure of our culture in its word tasks has brought about, in the last fifteen years, substantial expansion of research and interest in all aspects of communication. The sudden popularity of the field makes it appear like a new science; yet few philosophers, beginning with the Greeks and Hebrews, have developed their systems without some reference to the social nature of man and the ways of his relationship.

This is especially true of the Christian church, whose origins and history have been characterized and maintained by close, intimate association of its adherents. Its overarching doctrine of reconciliation, however defined, remains a communicative act, whether performed by God within the world, or enacted by the Holy Spirit through the life of Christians.

Much about communication has proved to be researchable. There is little we have not learned about its overt forms, and much has been discovered about its more deep-lying characteristics. However, one is increasingly convinced that, at the moment, no experimental design is capable of tapping the subtle emotional movement we call love, which is communication's most desired form and goal. Yet it is precisely to this problem that any Christian interpretation of communication must ultimately address itself.

In this book, attention is given to the person who, as a Christian, must carry on dialogue with his world. Being Christian, he communicates at the level of love, where the dynamics of his processes are hard to describe, and harder to define. It is possible, however, to observe the Christian as he structures his interpersonal relationships, and from these, work into some understanding of the fund of emotion that motivates him. It is assumed here that all communication is interpersonal encounter. Normative behavior for the Christian is a *loving* spirit, the matrix out of which all his communication arises.

Dealing with such material in book form places the writer under the handicap of using only one (and not the best) form of communication. Love requires all the means of relationship to describe it fully, and long periods of association to authenticate it. It is hoped, however, that the following chapters will provide some guidelines for re-evaluating the role of the Christian as a communicator.

Encouragement and help in preparing these pages came from more sources than I can mention. Under a Faculty Fellowship grant from the Sealantic Fund and the American Association of Theological Schools, I was permitted a year's leave from my teaching responsibilities. During this period I began this work. Upon my return to United Seminary, President Walter N. Roberts granted me every freedom I needed to complete the manuscript. Mrs. Eltha Horner was both skillful and patient in working my manuscript into final typewritten form. To all these I am indebted.

My family became accustomed to my excuses for not sharing many events with them. They should know, however, that whatever insights concerning Christian communication appear here have been deepened in my own life because of them.

H. A. DeW.

Dayton, Ohio

Chapter I

Communication and Christian Responsibility

Currently a great deal of attention is being given to how and why people need one another. We need to speak, listen, control, be controlled, and share. Almost everything has become too difficult for the person to accomplish alone, so we function in groups, both large and small, to do the things that are too hard for individual enterprise. This has created a prevailing mood that is characterized by an interest in people and their behavior. We have an insatiable desire to be related to one another, and these associations are carried on in countless ways, ranging from friendly and intimate contacts to planned complexities of mass production and communication. Some of these relationships are intense, formal, and purposive; others are relaxed, informal, and aimless.

The Sources of Concern

Such human association with all its attending problems is as old as man himself, but he has not always deemed it necessary to spend much time analyzing it. Therefore, with the sudden rise of interest in communication and human relations, one might well ask whether something has been wrong, for when people become more than casually attentive to some aspect of their existence, more than likely they are worried about themselves. Admittedly, our interest in communication has gained considerable impetus from scientific investigation in the field, but our concerns are derived just as much from the fact that our human relations are showing signs of wear and, in many instances, breaking down altogether.

That the church should also become interested in this development is not surprising. If communication is defined as the encounter of person with person, it is upon this precept that Christianity is structured and maintained. Moreover, a considerable terminology has been developed to describe aspects of the process – "witnessing," "evangelizing," "admonishing," "spreading the word," "edifying," "teaching," "exhorting," "proclaiming," "testifying," "preaching," etc. During its long history, the church has accepted the fact that it must tell something about its life and meaning, both within its own fellowship, and within the world.[1]

Indeed, it must be admitted that a great deal of such witnessing is actually taking place. The activity of the churches and the amount of time and space given to religion through mass media seem convincing enough as evidence that the church is doing its work of maintaining its life and confronting the world with a testimony to God's revealed Word. In fact, there should be some consolation in the fact that Christianity is newsworthy, and we are tempted to exercise some caution lest our publicity become a substitute for more thoroughgoing methods. A more alarming fact, however, is that the majority of Christians are not engaged in anything that even faintly resembles the mass productivity of the church. It is only a few who carry the burden of reaching the multitudes through these media or even through the planned programs of the church. The others – including both laity and clergy – maintain active participation in the life of the church, but in bearing testimony to the world, seem to manifest what amounts to a widespread loss of nerve.

It is to this problem that this book is directed. Upon the individual Christian rests the responsibility for communicating the gospel if it rests upon the church at all. As Christians, we are not talking about our Christian convictions in our contacts with the world. To be sure, we easily become involved in serious discussion and even arguments about "religion," but that

Christians are seriously concerned about witnessing to the love of God and actually proclaiming its availability to elevate the relationships between people seems open to question. How can the Christian communicate the faith? What are the methods of communication? What is the Christian's "way" with his world?

This is by no means a new problem to the church. From the outset, the followers of Jesus have had ample instruction in how to act and give reason for their faith. He gave them what today would be called "clinical training" in the process of encounter with the world (see especially Matt., ch. 10). He was the author of one of the most classic postulates of communication when he said, "Let what you say be simply 'Yes' or 'No'; anything more than this comes from evil."

From this beginning, the church continued to give instruction to its people as to how they should conduct themselves in the presence of others. With all their interest in formulating a systematic doctrine for the church, the early fathers were also concerned about methodology. This is especially true in the writings of Clement of Alexandria. His work, *Christ the Educator*,[2] should have wide reading among those interested in Christian education and evangelism. He was one of the first to translate the teachings of Jesus into the context of intimate human behavior. He instructs the Christian about his deportment in such things as eating, clothing himself, using jewelry, and in how to speak, about which he has this to say:

> Before you hear, answer not a word. A muffled voice is the voice of an effeminate man; however, the speech of a temperate man is moderate in tone, not too loud nor too long, not too quick nor too verbose. We should not be long-winded in our conversations, nor wordy, nor engage in idle chatter, nor rattle on rapidly without drawing a breath. Surely, even the voice ought to have its share, so to speak, of moderation, and those who talk out of turn and those who shout should be silenced. . . . A man full of tongue is terrible in his destruction. The rest of the body of a chatterer is worn away like an

> old shoe by evil, with only the tongue left to inflict harm. Therefore, wisdom advises us well: "Be not full of idle words in a multitude of ancients." Again, he seeks to eliminate idle chatter even in our relations with God by imposing restraint with this command, "Repeat not the word in your prayers." [3]

As the church fell within the orbit of the Roman Empire, however, all this was changed. Personal witness seemed pointless. The church was a *fait accompli.* Its people were the instruments of its support and enhancement. It did its own speaking through organizational representatives, and the individual was to glorify it; and, through it, glorify God. He was lost in this subtle form of mass communication and never entertained a feeling of responsibility for personal confrontation in the world.

Among other things that were reborn in the Reformation as it moved to refine and purify the church was the re-establishment of a personal religious integrity. This is nowhere more clearly declared than by Martin Luther in his treatise on *Christian Liberty,*[4] in which he sets down two of the fundamental principles along which the Reformation developed, and which, in turn, gave new impetus to the individual Christian as a communicator. These propositions are (1) "A Christian man is a perfectly free lord of all, subject to none" and (2) "A Christian man is a perfectly dutiful servant of all, subject to all." [5] Thus began a genuine interest in breaking apart the prevailing "mass-mindedness" that had characterized the church. The Wesleyan, Quaker, and Evangelical movements of the succeeding centuries laid stress upon the need for personal Christian responsibility. In 1853 *The Religious Telescope* printed this short injunction under the title "How to Admonish":

> We must consult the gentlest manner and the softest seasons of address. Our advice must not fall like a violent storm bearing down and making those to droop whom it is meant to cherish and refresh. It must descend as the dew upon the tender herb or like the melting flakes of snow. The softer it

> falls the longer it dwells upon and the deeper it sinks into the mind. If there are so few who have the humility to receive advice as they ought, it is often because there are few who have the discretion to convey it in a proper vehicle, and to qualify the harshness and bitterness of reproof against which corrupt nature is apt to revolt, by an artful mixture of sweetening and agreeable ingredients. To probe the wound to the bottom with all boldness and resolution of a good spiritual surgeon and yet with all the delicacy and tenderness of a friend requires a very dexterous and masterly hand. An applicable deportment and a complacency of behavior all disarm the most obstinate, whereas if instead of calmly pointing out their mistake we break out into unseemly sallies of passion, we cease to have an influence.[6]

Even without the refinement of current knowledge in the field of human relations, this shows some insight into the way of the Christian with his world. But what has happened to make it appear that the Christian is no longer an admonisher, a witness, or a communicator?

The Current Problem

First of all, during the past two generations, the churches have been moving toward a new form of "re-establishment." The growth of stronger and larger denominational groups tends to create impressive and highly organized administrative systems, raising in the minds of people some doubt as to the legitimacy of the individual and the small church body as adequate communicators. Along with this "re-establishment" goes a surrendering of many functions of the Christian life to the denomination or "authoritative" church body. Of course, much communication is surrendered also. It is the "large body" that publicizes its life, speaks for the people, places its approval upon the ways in which the world shall be confronted. The individual has developed a loyalty to his denomination, but in so doing, has increasingly lost – to planned programs, established curriculums, and agreed-upon procedures – the spontaneity for witness characteristic of the Christian.

Secondly, and as an added aspect of the first point, in spite of a great deal of evidence to the contrary, it is still true that the distance between the professional communicator of the Christian faith and the nonprofessional is wider than it should be. As the clergy become more and more educated, as theological dogma becomes more and more refined, and as this dogma continues to be the subject of countless Sunday morning sermons, the laity come to feel rather alien to it and hopeless in contemplating their task of testifying to it. They depend upon the clergy themselves to witness to the gospel and refer to them anything that suggests the need for interpretation of this gospel.

In the third place, Christians can gain vicarious satisfaction from hearing the media of radio, television, and mass proclamation witness to the gospel. Reading about or being spectators to the mass religious efforts of our age makes us happy in the thought that we have adequate people to represent us and speak the truth about God to the world. This kind of satisfaction leaves us feeling that the responsibility for communicating the faith is assumed, even though we do not share in it personally.

In the fourth place, the church may well be open to the criticism that in becoming a subculture of our society, it has developed a specialized language and unique forms of behavior that are not always understood within the fellowship nor readily communicated to people outside. We should not be too ready to discount this accusation until we take a hard look at the way things are with us. Even in a day when we advertise our friendly policy regarding all groups of people, still there are large masses with whom the church has little or no direct relationship. As groups develop, their values become more and more specific, and in turn, become less translatable to those outside the groups.

In the fifth place, it is quite possible that the responsibility for communicating the gospel is being bypassed simply because Christians do not have very much to say. There is serious question, for instance, as to whether the training we receive in the normal development of our Christian faith either confronts us with a satisfactory methodology necessary to bear our witness, or even encourages us to feel that such activity is important. One must have admiration for groups whose adherents are impelled to engage in deliberate personal encounter for the purpose of witnessing. Although they might not always consider it important to master the subtleties and refinements of their interpersonal activity, they are nonetheless making an assumption about their Christian lives that should bring other Christians to sharp attention – that communicating the gospel is so much a part of our personal religious experience that we cannot avoid its implications for our lives.

Some Basic Presuppositions

It is the basic presupposition of this book that the communication of the gospel is a personal responsibility derived from the nature of the gospel, and not merely a consequence of it. It is discourse as well as doctrine, method as well as content. The Christian faith is a special *way* things are accomplished, and a unique *way* relationships are carried on. The gospel implies that love is more than a "free-floating" concept; it is a principle of life that governs the affairs of people, and in turn, matures as people act it out in their daily affairs. It is the condition under which God functions and acts upon his people, and consequently, the highest human *event.* Since love has something to say about the way we gesture toward one another, it is only natural that Christians should become interested in the field of communication. Moreover, it is inevitable that the growing interest in the church will offer increasing opportunity for the development of a conscience concerning personal witnessing.

The Right to Communicate as a Person

Look again at the propositions of Martin Luther. He is speaking to and about the Christian man. The word "man" cuts through the many layers of clerical and priestly office, touching the human being as a person, the medium through which God has always sought to convey his word. We communicate the gospel as persons apart from our designations as pastor, church official, teacher, or any functionary appointed to perform the work of the church. Judgment falls first upon the person and the way he views his freedom and accepts his responsibilities. If man is "a free lord of all," it is then assumed that liberty is granted to all the capacities of human nature, even to the right to communicate.

We have this right to communicate, first of all, because we are human and born with amazing powers of self-extension. We probe the hidden precincts of matter, explore the resistant areas of the universe, and constantly maintain a relationship of curiosity with our environment. Overshadowing these obvious forms of adventure is our love of penetrating the lives of other people. We have an almost irrepressible desire to know people and to know about them. Psychology has become a ready ally in this adventure and makes the exploration of human life seem more respectable. To sever the bonds of communication drives us into a state of aloneness that we cannot tolerate. As if to establish ultimate protection, we have built an impressive network of signals, signs, and responses. By these we carry on our work, play, and worship. If, for some reason, the network is broken or even disturbed, we become anxious and bring into play all sorts of substitute devices to re-establish contact.

Even in situations where we seem to be guaranteed the greatest freedom, we are still bound by some serious limitations upon speech and action. Every culture, large or small, eventually develops its own ground rules for communication. Our speech is a good case in point. People must confine themselves to English where no other language is spoken. On the surface, confinement to a single language does not seem like an unsurmountable restriction, but how often do we want to express a feeling for which no word seems completely appropriate? The author and scholar must frequently reach into other languages and dialects for words for which his own tongue has no equivalent. We even embellish our words with gestures, loudness, and sometimes profanity, just because we want to say more than our language permits.

The culture man develops places even more subtle limitations on his right to communicate. The ground rules become more complicated when the boundaries between people become permeable, and we soon learn to distinguish what is right and proper to say and what is better left unsaid. Even the child soon learns the distinction between "public" and "private" speech, and the person who brings "private" speech into the ears of the public violates the taboo and is considered ill-mannered or even crude. For instance, in the course of casual conversation, to ask a person how much money he has in the bank would cause considerable embarrassment.

Moreover, cultures develop their own way of "looking at things." They develop systems of values and belief that control the communication among people. Traditions and law become something sacred, and therefore meaningful. They are upheld and restated by all groups in the culture. The individual speaks and acts within this belief system, and if he should choose to separate himself from it, he can do so without jeopardizing his position only as long as he does not violate the basic tenets of the culture.

A further complication develops as the culture breaks down into subcultures, of which there are many, and all of which develop their own language. Service clubs, lodges, the citizenry of Texas, labor unions, the churches, and the thousands of voluntary groups in our society set up their own standards of communication. For some, the person must know a special language to be admitted. In all of them the person can feel at home only when he has "mastered the language" and is able to enter freely into the conversation. This, in itself, is one level of man's "right to communicate." It is the unusual person who does not belong to some group in which he has the right to speak – his community, his home, his job, his circle of friends.

His very sense of belonging depends upon his ability to claim the right to reach out for association and participate in the speaking, listening, writing, and reading that goes on around him. Just so long as his psychophysical being is what it is, man's right to be a free participant in this world must be assured.

The Right to Communicate as a Christian

The Christian's right to communicate is determined, in the second place, by the nature of his religion. Luther's presuppositions about the freedom of man brought to light a principle laid down by the advent of the gospel. For many centuries clerics had maintained such logical and legal control over the church and over the religious lives of men that the declaration of Luther sounded new and even strange. However, it was the "sleeping giant" of the church. It declared that in the soul of man resides a spiritual power that is mediated there by the Holy Spirit, and established as the prerogative of all Christians by God's ultimate communicative act in sending his Son into the life of the world, "that in every way you were enriched in him with all speech and all knowledge . . . so that you are not lacking in any spiritual gift" (I Cor. 1:5, 7).

How does the right to communicate as a Christian differ from one's right to communicate as a human being? Is not the Christian bound by the same limitations of language and culture? Does not his communication break down because he must live and function with the rigid human patterns? Admittedly, the Christian is trained by his language and culture and must therefore speak, listen, and act within it, but it is also true that the Christian spirit offers man a language and skill that speaks above any language or culture man has devised.

> The power of which we speak is spiritual. It rules in the midst of enemies and is mighty in the midst of oppression, which means nothing else than that strength is made perfect in weakness, and in all things I can find profit unto salvation, so that the cross and death itself are compelled to serve me and to work together with me for my salvation. This is a

> splendid prerogative and hard to attain in a true omnipotent power, a spiritual dominion, in which there is nothing so good and nothing so evil but that it shall work together for good to me if I only believe. Lo, this is the inestimable power and liberty of Christians.[7]

Even though the Christian's right to communicate is defined in spiritual terms, it does not mean that we can avoid dealing with the strictures of language and culture. In later chapters, the obstacles to communication will be discussed more fully, but since the consideration of the rights of the Christian to communicate is so basic, some understanding of the restriction under which it functions will be helpful. Language, of course, stands in the way of both man-as-man and man-as-Christian. If, on the other hand, by language we mean the full range of expression of which man is capable, then man-as-Christian has access to a language of universal scope, unrestricted by either speech or culture. It is the language of being as well as doing, arising from a fund of spiritual information that is communicated in every contact. It is the value system along which words and gestures move; it is characterized by " love, joy, peace, patience, kindness, goodness, faithfulness, gentleness, self-control " (Gal. 5:22–23).

Even for man-as-Christian, however, the " right " to witness is limited by the language of the culture. The church as a " subculture " has developed a wide range of customs and language. For the clergyman, the right to speak from his fund of spiritual insight is sometimes frustrated by the need to speak from the language and customs of both church and society, and also by the weight of Christian dogma within which he speaks. To speak " beyond " this profound residue of the church's life and thought, and with a " different " language, either fills him with anxiety because of his inadequacy or lays him open to the charge of heterodoxy. He may feel no conflict here; but if he does not, he then has done exactly what man-as-man usually does, communicating and witnessing within bounds where language and thought are not threatening. His language will be accepted. He will have the sense of belonging, and demands will not be made of him beyond his culture.

For the layman, the threat of language is similar but with some additional problems. He too is the product of both church and culture, but by vocational choice must live in the world to a degree not required of the clergy. He is strongly influenced by his neighborhood and work groups, which have provided a home where he is permitted to assert his right to communicate. He might even be willing to take the church into the world by standing against prevailing evils without fear of losing either his right or his status in the group. For him it is a well-defined territory. He is opposed to corruption, injustice, and immorality, and wanting to be found on the side of the right, he enters into the network of communication to correct the ills and maintain the values agreed upon by his group. There is hardly a person who cannot lay claim to such action as this in some group where he holds membership, be it his own home, labor union, school board, or public government.

It has been assumed that the layman was best carrying on his witness by participating in this type of community enterprise, and it would be folly to discount its value. The question still remains open, however, as to whether this is the ultimate we can achieve in our Christian witness. Do we have the right to do more? The church has not always been helpful in answering this question. If its language is sometimes difficult to the clergy, for the layman it is downright confusing. In spite of long years of training in schools of the church, the theological main stream stands unrelated to his life in areas other than the church. Theological thought is not our stock in trade. We respect it and have a great respect for those who have developed it. We even feel the "rightness" and value of it; but without the necessary training, it is lost upon us, and we cannot claim the right to give something we cannot make our own.

If the layman finds it difficult to incorporate the language of the church into his everyday affairs, his problem is intensified by an uncertainty regarding his status before the clergy. In spite of the fact that Protestantism has structured its life and work on democratic principles, there are still many practices in the church that educate the layman to feel " under and separate " in relation to the clergy. The psychological setting of the Sunday morning worship service is a case in point. The minister is elevated. He is separated from the layman by a pulpit (usually made of hard wood), chancel railing, and a few rows of empty pews. The years of experiencing such a distance cannot help developing a feeling of inferior status that will manifest itself in many ways. In groups involving ministers the layman will be reluctant to communicate. He will not be quick to offer the witness of his own spiritual urges, and he may even distrust their validity.

What is more significant, the layman is even more doubtful of his right to communicate the gospel beyond the confines of the church. He lives in two worlds: the world of his church and the world of his culture. The first might help him negotiate the second, but the two cannot carry on a conversation through him. This condition cannot be attributed entirely to the layman's timidity or his lack of responsibility. The fact is, that in view of his unfamiliarity with the theological language of the church, and his uncertain status as a witness, he simply does not presume the right to communicate the gospel.

Both clergy and laity will need to interpret for themselves Luther's proposition on freedom. They are " perfectly free lords of all " with no qualification or status before God except that they be people of God whose name is Christian, who speak a language born of the activity of God's spirit in the soul. What Luther has established has been of primary concern in recent ecumenical conferences. The Amsterdam conference called for an " apostolate-by-fact " – a term taken from an article " 'Plot' of the Didache," by Prof. William Telfer, in *The Journal of Theological Studies* in 1947 (Vol. 45, July-Oct., p. 126).

> It does not depend on any commission or authorization by the church. Its motive force is simply the sense that Christ must everywhere be preached, and pity for the intolerable tragedy

that any man should die in ignorance of the glorious gospel that Christ has died for all. It is taken for granted that every Christian will have such a knowledge of the truth as to be able to give a reason for the faith that is in him; to defend that faith when it is attacked; to set it forth persuasively when opportunity offers; to present the challenge to personal decision without which the hearer, even when attracted by the gospel, may escape its implications for himself; to carry that infectious sense of joyfulness and victory, which in the majority of cases is the generative power of conversion; and to guide the neophyte through the difficult stages of temptation and disheartenment, which nearly always follow on the acceptance of the gift of God in Christ.[8]

Communication as Christian Responsibility

To establish the freedom to communicate fulfills only one aspect of the Christian's role as a witness to the gospel. In addition to his being a " free lord of all," Luther has added that " a Christian man is a perfectly dutiful servant of all, subject to all."

He tells us we are:

> not only . . . the freest of kings, we are also priests forever, which is more excellent than being king. Thus Christ has obtained for us, if we believe on him that we are not only his brethren, co-heirs and fellow beings with him, but also fellow priests with him, who may boldly come into the presence of God in the spirit of faith and cry " Abba, Father," pray for one another, and do all things which we see done and prefigured in the outward and visible works of priests.[9]

To be free to communicate the gospel without assuming the responsibility of doing so puts Christians in danger of seeking out a place of safety in our favored group without engaging in normal human encounter, or pushing outward the borders of the church through our witness. To be free gives us a comfortable feeling, and our first energies are spent generally in maintaining this security. Our language becomes more and more unintelligible to the world, and we can communicate only with those who share our group life and understand our speech. As F. W. Dillistone has pointed out, Rudolf Bultmann's declaration that the gospel is "independent of any picture of the world," is mainly of man's own making.[10] If there is a "great gulf fixed" between the gospel and the world, it is not because the gospel is not for the world, but because the Christian has chosen to make it so. We have exploited our rights to the full, even to the point of separating God's people and seriously impairing the lines of communication. Beyond the freedom to speak lies the reminder of Paul that we are to be regarded "as servants of Christ and stewards of the mysteries of God" (I Cor. 4:1). How do we become such servants and stewards?

First of all, the Christian will need to take a fresh look at himself as a Christian. He will need to see himself as a datum of the faith. Regardless of how strong the organized church becomes, and how well the gospel is preached and sent out to all people through other media, it nonetheless remains for the Christian to ask himself, "What role do I play in this task of communication?" We need to see ourselves not only as a people of God in the plural sense, but as a person of God in the singular sense. Although there is both strength and value in the ability of the church to speak with one voice, this should never becloud the fact that God's "person" will continuously ask, "What is it that I, and I alone, must say?" The Christian needs to re-examine the resources of his life and take a look at his personality as an instrument of God's planning and will. We should not be afraid to face ourselves directly with the assurance that whatever provides for the ultimate transmission of the gospel of Christ to other people resides in the single person. For what is done collectively, although it appears in greater and more powerful form, can likewise be accomplished within the framework and capacities of the individual person.

This does not mean that we should look at ourselves as virtuous and complete, for we shall find that all communication, whether it has to do with the gospel or with any other cultural subject, proceeds not from a clear voice from God through channels that are unobstructed by our own needs, but rather proceeds on the direct basis of our own needs, and is filtered through the many impressions we have of our world and the particular ways in which we have been taught to confront our world. The Christian, even though he be a person of God, is still a person and must face himself frankly on this basis, being neither ashamed nor overconfident about what he sees, freely accepting the fact that as a communicator, even of the holy things of God, he is subject to all the vicissitudes of human behavior.

In the second place, the Christian must be responsible for making himself intelligent about the meaning of communication. Probably we do not like to admit that the one last stronghold of independent action is now being the subject of scrutiny by the scientists. Talk, and especially talk with friends in a casual, offhand manner, should certainly be free from scientific investigation. Let the scientist examine the atom and let him probe outer space, but when it comes to poking around in our close relationships, and especially those so personal to us as our talk, we are led to think that the scientist has become an intruder. However, it is all-important that we give much time to examining what happens when we come into one another's presence, especially since this is the area in which there is great misunderstanding and serious breakdown. Moreover, it has been suggested that only through the study of communication can we find a single system whereby human behavior can be understood.[11]

The Christian must raise such questions as: How do I sound to other people? What do the words I say mean to others? What should I expect to happen when I confront other people? At what point are people ready to hear the things of religion? How can I understand what they are thinking of me and what I am saying to them? What are some of the guidelines by which the behavior that I manifest in the casual and everyday experiences of life can be measured?

This would be a good place to examine some of the basic

tenets of communication. It should be understood that there is no magic in the word "communication" itself. It is not the panacea for all our ills. It is nothing more nor less than simply the transmitting of a signal from one person to another, who understands this signal and makes an appropriate response. The signal is not necessarily verbal, but includes the whole range of human activity so that "where the relation of (human) entities is considered, we deal with the problem of communication." [12] It can be given by persons for the most evil of intents. Even though there is no honor among thieves, hardly the same can be said of communication. We are under an illusion if we expect communication per se to be a healer. It is not even self-repairing when it breaks down. It is not true that simply by talking, gesturing, listening, and writing our problems of human association will be solved. It is not even enough to understand and to make sure that we are understood. We have learned enough about human nature to know that persons can well understand the dangers they face and yet deliberately walk into them, or understand the needs of others and deliberately avoid them.

This is exactly why, within the last two decades, there has been a growing interest in the dynamics of human interaction. Industry, education, government, social welfare, and the world of entertainment have been looking to the social psychologist in an effort to determine the nature of the forces at work when people relate to one another and set out to affect one another. Why do some relationships succeed and others fail? How are individual characteristics involved in our interpersonal processes? Why is it that some groups cannot talk to one another without deepening the rift between them? What makes a person most likely to "get along" with others? Studies of these questions have helped us improve our skills and communications. They have given the salesman, the statesman, the executive, and the therapist, and even the religionist, new insights in dealing with people. They have helped us move deeper and deeper into the lives of people, and we have even reached the extreme where advertising now threatens to tinker with our subconsciousness.

However great the progress has been in the development of communication skills, there is still a persistent feeling among scientists that much cannot be known. No scientist is able to describe the varied and subtle forces that have stimulated persons into action, or all the responses a person might make in a situation. A hurried glance at the countless relationships in which we function as Christians will convince us that, difficult as it is, if we can develop an art whereby our approach to other people becomes more refined and more expertly handled, we shall not only improve the quality of our witness, but we shall become much more effective as persons in the whole range of our experiences with others. We are church school teachers, church officials, organization officers, choir members, participants in the life of the church in one way or another, and in addition, we carry on a multitude of quasi-religious functions in our homes and communities where we work and play. The number of face-to-face contacts in these endeavors is enormous, and offers the Christian unlimited opportunity to make religious profession a part of our lives. The Christian, therefore, has the responsibility to learn how to talk, listen, respond, and gesture toward the other person. Learning this process somehow is not accomplished the same way we learn to do other things – spot airplanes or become an accountant, for instance. It is an art, and art is developed only through practice and constant attention to the way we perform in relation to our concept of God. It is this kind of art, therefore, that the Christian needs to achieve.

In the third place, the Christian must be responsible for determining how his Christian convictions bear upon the way he develops his communication skills. Can the resources of science describe completely the dynamics of communication, or are there certain aspects of human relations which do not yield to measurement procedures? The scientist is concerned mainly with trying to determine what dynamics are at work in the processes of communication, what kind of communication makes for better human relationships, and he is concerned with trying to draw a line between smooth and nonsmooth working out of the incidents in which people attempt to affiliate with one another. He does not ask the question, "What is Christian or what is un-Christian?" about what is going on. This is left for the Christian to do; and the more one looks at the claims of the Christian gospel, the more one is impressed with the great amount that has been said regarding the simple give-and-take of everyday life, and the way in which the Christian must respond to it.

No matter how well we are able to incorporate into the life of the church such skills that will draw crowds, increase the budget, and even make the transmission of our religious language a thing of ease, we cannot claim the right to communicate as Christians unless we raise the fundamental questions as to what purposes these skills are to serve. Do they proclaim the gospel? Do they raise the question of man's life and destiny; his place before God? Do they earnestly seek to protect the integrity of those to whom we bear the gospel? Do they result merely in maintaining and building the church as a closed order that stands apart from the world, or do they establish contact with persons and groups so desperately in need of Christ's redeeming power? To raise such questions lifts communication to a new and different level. Its processes are enlivened by a spiritual power that guides the communicator not only in the way he speaks but also for what purpose.

The Direction of the Christian Witness

The Christian must also answer the question as to where he does his speaking and to whom he witnesses. Christians have had phenomenal success in building and maintaining their own fellowships, but

> Danger threatens where we draw our strength from the Word of God, live by it, feel ourselves to be vulnerable against the intrusion of the "other," but have ceased to struggle amid the

> confusion of tongues around us. Before we know it our lives and our way of speaking are caught up in a great wave of traditionalism, and our faith becomes rigid. Believers withdraw into their own circle and no longer stand in the fullness of life. They give a special place in their lives to the fostering of their own inner being, and live in their distinctly marked fellowship. The introverted language, unintelligible in the world, is only an indication of a process that is extremely disquieting.[13]

This danger goes even deeper. The Christian is handicapped by being encouraged to develop two languages. On the one hand, within the fellowship he speaks the language of tradition spoken among people who understand the clichés, and he returns them in kind. The church is no exception to the principle that language and tradition feed on each other. Any group of people, large or small, binds itself together by means of words, symbols, and gestures that are mutually understood. As the understanding grows, the language in turn changes to accommodate the new-found relationships, and eventually, it is understood only by those who are properly initiated.

On the other hand, the Christian has a " world " language. He uses it outside the church. It too is the language of tradition, binding together people in the pursuits of community life. There are symbols, gestures, and even beliefs that accompany the language. They are necessary to maintain the educational, occupational, and recreational activities of the community. These are broken down into smaller groups with their own forms of communication, so that the person speaks one language in his church on Sunday, another at work during the week, and still another in the group he seeks out for his other community interests. Thus, man is usually multilingual and communicates within many networks. He is a Christian (more likely designated by the denomination to which he belongs), a democrat, a worker, a father, and a member of his community group.

Although this could develop confusion in an individual, it

generally does not. Man's health depends upon a point of reference, a center of life and thought, which dominates all aspects of his activity. He cannot long tolerate being broken apart by conflicts at the center of his life. He yearns for integration, wholeness, and a single voice. As a part of his education, therefore, he develops his own private language. He generally takes it over from one or more of the groups to which he belongs, but it will be truly his own. Just as surely as each person develops his own personality characteristics, so we develop our system whereby our personality is communicated. In spite of the long drive toward this individuality, we take our cues from the most significant groups in our life. No one ever completely loses contact with the communication system with which he was involved in his own home, for instance. We speak what our parents spoke in us. As we grow up and broaden our group association, we get the "feel" of other languages and new communication systems. We either reject them or embrace them, depending on how easily we can incorporate them into the already existing systems. Eventually, however, a dominating style overtakes us. We form a set of beliefs which hold us together. This becomes our traditional self with its own language and its own ways of communication. It is a closed system of meaning. If others cannot understand us, we like to believe we can understand ourselves.

Since we pass through the hands of many teachers, and most of them more impressive than the church, it is little wonder that our lives and language are dominated by a worldly culture, and that the dialogue between the Christian and the world flows inwardly and not outwardly. It is little wonder that we must constantly ask why the world does not listen when we speak! Too often when the Christian speaks to the world he speaks not as a Christian but as a man of the world who has embellished his concepts with religious phraseology. He feels satisfied to introduce into his world as much religion as the group can tolerate. A kind of training goes on between church and world. The church receives proved administrative and organizational practice in return for some broad and ethical guidelines for social behavior and for short "worship services," or a "word of prayer" as adjuncts of community gatherings. To take seriously his responsibility as a communicator of the gospel, the Christian must re-evaluate his role in this scheme of things. He will need to ask what is in truth dominating his life.

The Christian as Theologian

In the fourth place, the Christian has the responsibility of lifting his nonprofessional status as a theologian into an aura of respectability. If one of the causes for the breakdown of individual concern for the speaking of the gospel is found in the fact that much of our Christian interpretation of life has been taken over by the theologian, it then becomes our task to reinstate every person as a priest and theologian in his own right. This will not be easy, for theology has gained a tremendous amount of respectability and status in our religious culture, and anyone who dares enter into it must almost automatically change his status from the nonprofessional to the professional. The church has always needed to deal with division of responsibility in its life. On the one hand, there are those designated to do the work of the church (pastors, missionaries, and appointed lay workers). On the other hand, there are millions of Christians who have a witness to bear, but who feel an uncertain status in its communication. This has tended to increase the number of "preachers" among the laity, and it has become traditional for the layman to think that when and if he reaches a certain level of understanding and professionalism about theology, he must become ordained or receive certain "credentials" from the church.

There is some question as to whether this is normative for the Christian who is the "perfectly dutiful servant of all." The Christian interested in bearing individually the testimony to God's truth and developing his theological understanding becomes the communicator of the gospel when he relates what he knows to the life that he lives in his own vocation, whether clerical or lay. However true this may be, the nonprofessional is still under the necessity of making his position in the church of value and equated with the work done by the professional theologian. How can he speak if he doesn't know what to speak? How can he reach a level of understanding of the Christian faith unless he goes through the amount of training necessary to understand all these things? The answer does not lie in making a "professional" out of everyone, for in the true interpretation of professional theology, we find simply a development of what has been found to be true in the lives of the countless millions of Christians the world over. So, in reality, the lay person is a theologian when he begins to feel and think in terms of God, and God's revelation in Christ, and the presence of the Holy Spirit in the world. To be sure, he may not attach to this all the refinement and sophistication of theology itself, nor always put it into logical forms that can be readily understood by all the world. But every Christian must become an interpreter of God's will, and test his interpretation in an encounter within the fellowship and with the world. In this way he throws into the basket the apples that the professional theologian will sort over to produce the dogma most meaningful to the church. One of our greatest liabilities is that professional theology does not always represent the thinking of the Christian community nearly so much as it represents the thinking of a few persons who develop their theology out of highly personalized experiences. This means that the lay person should not be ashamed of his theological witness and should be responsible as a person in developing that witness to a level of respectability and adequate functioning.

In the fifth place, the Christian will be responsible for understanding what it means to live as a Christian among people. Communication is simply a means to an end. It holds us together and builds an understanding of the meaning of community and communitarian acts. It might well be said that communication is the tie between our present level of relationship and succeeding levels of relationship. If the association people have with one another is built and developed to new levels. it will be because the communication system has been sufficiently able to accomplish this. On the other hand, if the relationship between people tends to worsen, it is probably due to the breakdown of communication and to its lack of effectiveness.

Moreover, it can also be said that the very way we live together and feel toward one another has something to do with the type of communication that will be carried on. The soft, gentle, inviting words of the person will achieve certain things that harsh, demanding, angry words will not. Thus there is constant relationship between communication and the type of life that is lived, and it is this responsibility that the Christian will have to assume if the witness to Christ's love is to be carried on.

These, then, are the areas of responsibility in which the Christian must feel alerted if we are to develop a new insight into the Christian as a communicator. It is these responsibilities which will be developed more fully in the following chapters.

Chapter II

Christians Are Persons

Man is subject to all the laws of human nature, and though we are able to speak and understand a " language of the spirit," we neither hear nor speak it in pure form. It is heard, given meaning, and expressed within the range of human capacities. It is spoken with the words that one has at his command. These are uttered by one human being and heard by another. The hearer translates the words into his own spiritual language and they take on meaning for him. During this complex process of the transference of meaning from person to person, the signals and responses filter through countless influences, attitudes, feelings, and purposes – all of them human.

The Adequacy of Human Nature

Our humanity is in no way to be interpreted as a handicap in the process of communication. To be sure, we do not readily understand one another and we sometimes do not have the proper words and expressions satisfactorily to return the signals we receive, but our human nature, with all the attending inadequacies of speech, hearing, and gesture, possess tremendous possibilities for interaction with other people. Indeed, we must stand in awe of the fact that love, which is God's very nature, is freely and indiscriminately offered to man-as-man as a basis for his happiness and creativity. Moreover, it is not without significance that when God revealed himself in final form he did it within the framework of the Jesus' humanity. If we are able to tolerate the slow progress we make as Christians toward the development of our skills in communicating the gospel and if we are able to bring our expressive behavior under the direction of God's love, we shall come to find that this vessel he has given is a most adequate vehicle for the witnessing to his love in the world.

The Breakdown of Communication

Such an optimistic generalization about the possibilities of human nature should not hide the fact that we are always embarrassed by our failure to function as persons of God. Our communication is always somewhat disturbed and sometimes completely meaningless. Our inner needs are many and varied, and since their fulfillment depends, in most instances, upon other people, our fear of not having them met often makes us oblivious to the other person. He is not a part of our " event," and the relationship fails because it is not governed by mutual concern.

We fail also because there are so many varieties of communication to be mastered. I am indebted to Jurgen Ruesch for suggesting a list of the different communication channels common to everyday life.[14] In a paragraph he shows how it is possible for one person to participate in all forms during a given day. The following chart gives specific illustrations.

Activities	Type of Communication
Reading a letter Writing a note to the milkman	Written communication
Chatting with a neighbor Dictating a letter Listening to the radio	Speech communication
Teaching a church school lesson P.T.A. committee meeting	Group communication

Activities	Type of Communication
Studying a church school lesson Reading a novel	Communication through the printed word
Reading the newspaper Watching television Form letter from the church	Mass communication
Eating alone Meditation	Self-communication
The odor of dinner cooking Eyes burning in a smoky atmosphere	Chemical communication
Feeling fabric for quality Shaking hands with friends	Communication through touch
Congregational singing Swimming	Communication through action
The sanctuary altar Traffic signal light	Communication through symbol
Ambulance siren Church bell	Communication through sound
Monument to political leader Old church preserved for historical purposes	Communication through material culture
Looking through a mail-order catalog Using pictures to illustrate church school lesson	Pictorial communication
An evening at the theater Community drama	Communication through the arts

Even our repeated failures to communicate adequately will not prevent us from engaging in communication at every opportunity. The needs such activity satisfies are deeply written into human life. We shall do well to take a look at some of these needs to determine what communication means to us.

The Balance Between Curiosity and Comfort

In the first place, communication has some relation to man's need to find a satisfying balance between curiosity and comfort. These are reciprocal behavior patterns. We explore our world and familiarize ourselves with its signals – voices, sounds, signs, color, symbols. Our comfort is established by this visual-auditory intake. We feel reassured if the impulses we receive are not discordant, but let something unfamiliar slip into the accustomed patterns and we are brought to sharp attention. The mother who can sleep through all kinds of traffic noises will be awakened by the soft cry of her infant child. It is characteristic of our growing up to want to widen the boundaries of the areas where we feel free to communicate, and we shall even be willing to risk existing comforts to satisfy this curiosity.

Having grown up under influences that severely frowned upon the theater, I can well remember my first venture into a movie. I had done my best to make certain I would not be seen by the condemnatory eyes of my family and church, but I could not be at all certain I would escape the judgmental eyes of heaven. My guilt was enhanced when I found the inside of the theater an upended world, compared with the one I knew. I had never been anyplace where such a large group of persons was doing something in the dark. This fact, plus the antics on the screen of people I had been taught to distrust, made this a place of utter strangeness. I can now conclude that it was not so much the "sinfulness" of the event that impressed me as it was the unfamiliar, the different, the new-found setting with which I would need to establish a new communication pattern.

It is probably to our discredit that adventure such as this is to be confined to youth, for life moves quickly toward a stability within an environment in which both comfort and curiosity are satisfied. As this happens, our range and quality of communication become fixed, and life assumes a certain stationary value or function on the basis of what is sometimes called the "principle of least effort." [15] Since religious belief is so closely associated with personality need and growth, it is only natural we should look for need-fulfillment in the kind of religion and religious experience that will fit most closely the sounds and sight that are in keeping with our past history. In changing residence it is not infrequent that people "shop around" until a church is found to their liking. The words "to their liking" are filled with more insecurity about religion than we are willing to admit. They are reaching for a kind of religious community in which they are assured comfort (sounds, language, and gestures of others) and the need to explore (their own speech, sounds, and gestures.) This kind of communication holds us together as a Christian fellowship. The members make sounds and signs that are easily understood by everyone and accepted as their own. Therefore, a Christian fellowship can become more and more deeply involved in its own self-maintenance, and gradually become a rigid community into whose midst the outsider often finds it difficult to penetrate.

The glaring tragedy here is that the need to be curious has been stopped. The intake of material to the human body is cut off from the forces that guarantee growth and creativity. For the individual to stop the process of curiosity and search at the points where he can handle it and has no fear of being threatened is literally to cut off the activity of God within current history, and when people band themselves together on these premises it is done not without bringing serious judgment upon the Christian community. Here was one of the grievances Jesus had against the religious community of his day.[16] It could not be criticized for its lack of dogma or even its ability to stand against the inroads of pagan foreign power. What had happened to it, however, and what Jesus objected to in its life, was the fact that these people "strained" at their religious practices, and gave them meaning only within the context of earlier religious customs, which they sought to authenticate.

Individual Christians fall prey to this tendency. It is not simply accidental that our most frequent approach to people is an invitation to them to come to church with us. That is, our message to the world is not to minister to it, but rather to bring it within the orbit of our own comfort. Even the minister himself frequently is looked upon in his pastoral visitation as the promoter of church attendance and loyalty. When he appears at our doors we immediately think of the degree of our recent faithfulness in attending services, and if it has not been too commendable we immediately feel like apologizing for our not having been at church. In only too many cases this is the way the minister sees himself. All of this grows out of one of the most persistent needs of human nature: to find and construct the sort of world whose sounds, expressions, and sights will not be too confusing or threatening.

The Need to Extend and Express

Communication is carried on also in order to meet the needs of extension and expression. Human nature has a tremendous capacity to express itself. Man is able to extend his normal powers of voice to unbelievable distances. He can transmit his image around the world. Through clever machinery he is able to multiply his muscular energy to move mountains. As long as we have breath we are in a state of motion, and even our sleeping hours are a form of internalized activity.

This is especially true of one of the most important of our communicating apparatuses — the voice. We are chattering people. Clarence Day [17] has suggested that this is a "simian" world with the need to send verbal signals. Gardner Murphy adds that "Chatter is so important that we assemble in vast buildings the collection of canned or bottled chatter which the ages have accumulated." [18] Some learned people [19] use the term "chatter need" (*Schwatzbedürfnis*) to describe this array of collective social relationships which helps to dispel our loneliness. We are capable of speaking upward of twenty-five thousand words a day; mainly, I suspect, to fulfill this need to chatter. Moreover, we tend to be rather indiscriminate of the content with which we bombard our world. Speech often takes the form of unnecessary verbiage and we go to much greater lengths than necessary to express ideas. We are not persons of few words, and speak not always because we have something to say, but because we must be saying something.

The church is a speaking community, and its avowed purpose is to proclaim a message.

> O for a thousand tongues to sing
> My great Redeemer's praise,
> The glories of my God and King,
> The triumphs of his grace.

On any given Sunday morning the amount of words spoken and sung is rather surprising. Church school teachers, ministers, and others engaged in the affairs of building and maintaining the fellowship are all afforded opportunities to say what is on their minds. It is not surprising that recent trends in group dynamics have seemed to suggest that every person ought to be given a chance to express himself, whether he feels he wants to or not. Many persons operating in the fields of group work do not feel comfortable unless they have "full participation," and we have concluded that expression is somehow tied up with survival.

While this is undoubtedly true, we may forget that expression is many things and that man has many avenues through which he can "proclaim" the things of his life. He is not necessarily tied to his voice habits. Simply being in the group may be the only expression necessary from a given person, or lending an attentive ear a helpful form of expression. Our communication is based upon the desire to express ourselves, not only verbally but in all ways capable to the human make-up and structure.

The Need to Authenticate

A third need pushes a little more deeply. Man has an undying need to authenticate himself. The child is not in this world long before he discovers what is expected of him. Responsibilities are piled one on top of another until we reach adulthood, when we find we are husbands, wives, children, parents, accountants, dentists, members of the local school board, neighbors, each demanding specific obligations. As these are proved to be important to us, we need to invest our time authenticating them. So, as workers, we talk like workers, communicate as workers, and associate with those who reinforce our image of ourselves as workers. Thinking of ourselves as parents, we almost intuitively talk like parents, communicate with other parents, and in all ways possible take on the characteristics of parents.

The image of ourselves as Christians also needs authentication. Here the whole range of sounds, sight, and gesture combine to help us maintain our status as Christians. Holy days, our regularly scheduled services of worship, our understood rituals, everyday practices of our lives, and the moral aspects of our behavior remind us that the image we have of ourselves is being sustained. In very subtle ways our communication with others is an endeavor to win from them approval for our behavior as Christians. We expect to hear from the minister and from our church school teachers words that will reinforce our belief system. We do not mind being reminded of our failures within our Christian image, but we may revolt violently if we suspect the image itself is being tampered with.

As teachers and leaders in the Christian community we reaffirm ourselves in many ways. It is no secret that our teaching itself can easily reflect deep personal needs. It may even be a protection against too close scrutiny to our inner motivations and impulses. As long as we are able to verbalize in the presence of others, we are able to keep control of the direction of the formation of thoughts and ideas, and as long as we can keep them within realms that will give approval to our own basic thought patterns, it is well with us. Moreover, we may have here one of the reasons why it is so difficult for us to carry religion to the world. The non-Christian is somewhat like a child. He is apt to ask embarrassing questions. He is apt to level criticisms that we know are not entirely unfounded. He is apt not only to require of us proof of our own religious consecration and sincerity, but also to encourage us to defend the image of our Christian faith. In fact, we even express this by saying, "I am really not worthy to talk to others about Christianity," or "I have got to improve myself a great deal before I feel I can talk to someone else about Christ." These are honest opinions and we should not be too hard on ourselves for actually believing that we must reinforce our own personality structures. It is only when it becomes a continuous frustration to the carrying of God's word that the communication toward the reinforcement of ourselves becomes a serious handicap.

The Establishment of Social Space

A fourth area of personal need which our communication tends to meet is that of establishing the exact distance between ourselves and others. Very early in life, the child will soon distinguish between what is good in his environment and what is undesirable. He cannot feel warm and close to the undesirable mother. He will be uneasy and fretful. On the other hand, in the presence of the desirable mother he will come close and feel comfortable and let his whole body be absorbed into the loving one. From these very rudimentary beginnings we develop ever so gradually a process of learning exactly how much distance to put between ourselves and other people. It may be that as we grow we never permit others to come close to us until they have proved themselves to us, or until we have proved to ourselves that we can be comfortable in their presence. On the other hand, we may build up a very tolerant attitude toward people and move directly toward them, only grudgingly giving way to establishing this "social space" between them and us. It is here, probably, that our communication patterns serve us best. Our tone of voice, our gesturing, our glances, our very words, soon will tell people whether they are welcome or whether it is not good for them to get too near. If communicating the gospel depends upon warmth and closeness, if love operates only where people are able actually to impinge upon one another, then the matter of distance becomes important. And if our techniques of communication are such that they can establish distance with almost momentary rapidity, then it becomes important that we ask ourselves what our communication means in terms of this need to place distance between ourselves and others.

There is a deeper religious significance to this matter of distance. How we view other people has some relation to what we believe about God, about sin, the sinner, and our own righteousness. How close should we get to people? How much should we permit ourselves to be involved with people whose world and ways are frowned upon by the righteous community? What attitude should we take toward the sinner? Is it possible to differentiate between the sin and the sinner? And when we speak of the sin in derisive terms, does not this carry over to the sinner himself? When we become patronizing and attempt to become tolerant, even though we know in our heart we cannot be tolerant, are we not truly betraying our need to fulfill our theological concepts of other people's sinfulness and our righteousness? In order to establish its roots firmly in an unfriendly culture, the early church encouraged its people to "come apart," not to be equally yoked with unbelievers, to be one with the world and yet apart from it, to be "called persons," and felt it necessary to justify a certain "in-groupness" in the church. The present living church faces other needs. It is secure and accepted in our culture, and its influence can be felt everywhere. This now means that there should be no fear of losing our unique purpose in the world; hence, no need to maintain its "distance" from people. Indeed, its need now may be the very opposite – to close distances and to fill the social space with a Christian vitality and concern.

Such an intimate personal need must be dealt with at first hand if our communication is to have any effect. If there was one characteristic of Jesus that admits of no question in the minds of anyone, it is the fact that he was able to move freely among all conditions of men everywhere. His language was not a language of repetition and sameness; he did not have to mouth a constant reaffirmation of a faith for people. We get the impression that he was first interested somehow in giving his life. This meant he was able to close the distance between himself and other people at will, and permit his conversation and witness to the love of Almighty God be carried upon this closeness and upon this willingness to let his life be absorbed into the life of another. He did not seem to be in need of defending anything. In fact, he seemed to take great liberty with the things that the religionists tended to defend. To him a "defense of faith" was entirely contrary to the basic tenets of love, and was a necessary procedure only for those people who were in need of establishing good distance between themselves and other people. It is in this regard, probably, that Christianity has failed to free itself from a long history of a gradation of righteousness within the community. Even among the freest of sects and groups there is a continued distinction not only between clergy and laity but between saint and sinner, the churched and the unchurched. This does not mean, of course, that all the laity are overreacting to their own personal needs for maintaining adequate distance between themselves and others, nor does it mean that all Christians who enter the church and withdraw from society and from other people to perform their religious services and carry on their Christian action are guilty of deep-seated emotional and spiritual disturbance. It does mean, however, that we are ever reluctant to give up the badges of status that both authenticate ourselves and at the same time provide us with the amount of distance we need to maintain this.

This is no more clearly seen than among laymen who feel

impelled to lift the level of their witness in the world. They do so only after they have satisfied themselves they will be "acceptable." This is accomplished either by moving over into the professional ranks, or gaining the rank of a "lay preacher" and by engaging in quasi-professional activities. This has filtered down into all areas of our educational work and in our engrafting the young into society. Our educational processes in the church especially are filled with the maintaining of distance between teacher and child, between parent and child, between the advanced and the novice. It is felt that somehow the maintenance of this distance will give the person a challenge to move across it to become like ourselves, and the teacher feels he has no recourse other than to train those under him to become like himself. Not like himself as a person perhaps, but certainly like him in his thought world and in his image of what he knows and understands to be right and good.

To the degree that this happens, our communication suffers. Our words as well as our love and concern must be thrown across this distance. Love cannot then be established as a one-to-one relationship. It rather travels from one through a preconception of himself to another, and by the time it gets to the other it has lost its original and intended meaning. Very often this distance is used to control the communication event, and we become rather upset if those under us begin to move too directly, or too aggressively, toward us or toward one another. If they show "disrespect" for our status as teachers or leaders, we become a little unsettled, for to have people close the distance between themselves and us is not always considered to be a blessing within the educational system. Across this distance the love words are lost, as is the sacrificial act, for it is difficult to accept what others would do to us and demand from us. The distance prevents us from being an instrument of their growth. Rather, a whole new set of principles, quite unchristian in their basic assumptions, begin to function. We demand respect, and if we cannot get it as teachers, we get it through the wielding of a dogmatic and theoretical body of knowledge which contains in it a great many threats or promises of reward, which we hope will command the status that we are not able to feel as a human being. Our body of knowledge becomes a handy instrument. Not content to let dogma and ritual stand for themselves and speak for themselves, we cannot subject them to the rules and judgment of faith whereby all men are able to contemplate them and take from them what they need. The dogma or ritual becomes ourselves. We are dominated by it. It defends us, and our attempts to defend it are simply the maintenance of the supports that will sustain our distance from other people. Consequently, we offer people this dogma, this accretion of the thinking and life of the church, and withhold ourselves denying entrance of the Spirit of God between ourselves and others to formulate an interpretation of the meaning of life.

Communication Synonymous with Being

It is almost fashionable to think of human "need" as a negative phenomenon, and therefore assume that the person for whom "needs" are somehow unimportant or minimized is the only one capable of initiating a relationship whose purpose is to be helpful to another. This is often demonstrated in the Christian's denial of his ability to speak to others because of the persistence of his own problem. Little do we realize that we influence other people whether or not we make a special effort. Man does not simply *possess* the capacity to communicate. Rather, the very nature of our being is defined in terms of communication. Hardly any aspect of the physical or psychological make-up is free from involvement in the give-and-take with the world. Even the deepest meanings of life will sooner or later find their way through the surface into some sort of expression. It is just as though every visible aspect of man's personality were designed especially to engage in a dialogue with his environment. To be sure, this quality is shared with other beings, but the refinement of the process in man moves him far beyond the highest of the animal world.

By means of our communication apparatus, the world is bombarded with countless symbols and impressions and at the same time receives from it a great deal more than is ever realized. It is much like saying, " I am hungry." Hunger characterizes me. It designates the particular state of my being. It is hard to locate hunger in the body. It is diffused into all its parts. So it is with being Christian. To say, " I am Christian," is to say that my very being is beamed in the direction of a particular way of life. When we talk about compartmentalizing our lives in such a way so that we live out our Christian convictions in terms of our relationship to the church and then fulfill other responsibilities during the week in terms of our families and our jobs, we are not going deeply enough into the human personality to define it. No matter how hard we try to build a multiform personality, one phase of which is religion, we are entertaining a delusion. If we go deeply enough into our lives, we will find that these many forms are brought under one single guiding and dominating force, and this constitutes one's highest belief, and therefore one's religion.

Moreover, man exists in a " field." We are not isolated individuals but participants in a " situation-as-a-whole." The boundaries of this situation are indeterminate. No strict line separates individuals from one another. We move into the lives of people and they move into ours. The communicator stands in the center of his situation, the listener in the center of his. Without making any conscious attempt, our acts, our gestures, our words affect and control the world, words, signals, and responses of others. The communicative process is a movement because *being* itself is movement. It is this movement within the arena of the life of the world which characterizes man as a communicating being. We merely do not *possess* apparatus with which to communicate, but we *are* the communicating apparatus. It is helpful to look at this communication apparatus not so much in terms of the physical equipment we have at our disposal to perform these acts of communication, but rather in terms of the dynamics within the person who is in this give-and-take with his world.

Personality Dynamics and Communication

The first of these dynamics is that of sensing. A great many people would like to have long periods of peace and quiet, but little do we realize how much our well-being depends upon sensing things in our environment. Tests have shown that people cannot long tolerate a world in which they cannot sense what is going on about them. If their abilities to touch, smell, see, and hear are minimized, the body is soon crying for more association with its world. Even when persons who are extremely tired are brought into these experiments, at first they look forward to being in a situation where interference from the outside will be minimized, only to wake up within the hour with great discomfort, asking to have some contact with their world. Even when we are asleep, the subtle noises, faint light, and contact with pillow and pallet are important to us. The comfortable association of the body with the environment, the climate, the ability to hear the accustomed noises of our surroundings, the ability to see and to make judgments as to distance and size, are all so familiar to us that we do not realize how important they are to our ability to relate to our world.

It should be noted here that our ability to hear is one of the strongest and most deeply seated senses we have. It is probably the best protected of all our intake mechanisms. We are told that to have our hearing cut off is to remove one of the most important sources of spiritual sensitivity.[20] The ear detects the inflection, the innuendo, the sound of need, to a degree that the eye cannot do. Later on, the importance of this will be seen when we show how listening is an important aspect of our relationship to other people in witnessing to our faith. All that we sense is buried in a reservoir of meaning. The things we see, hear, and feel do not stay on the surface. None of them is lost; they become incorporated into the very fabric of our make-up. It is from these that the next step in the use of our apparatus for communication is taken.

The second dynamic is that of responding. Man has a fundamental need for reciprocal relationship with his environment. We cannot constantly be taking in. In some way or other we are going to utilize the things we have felt, heard, and seen. We cannot let them die as long as we are alive. It is important that we give an answer to the world, and although we will vary greatly in the way the response is made, respond we will. We must answer what has been sensed. The artist in his way, the poet in his, even the recluse in his way, are all giving answer to what they hear the world saying. So when the early church felt under obligation to admonish its adherents that they must carry this gospel into all the world, they were not introducing an element foreign to the dynamic make-up of the human personality. They were simply indicating what had been latent, even stunted, in the development of societies prior to that time; that is, an essential freedom within man to let himself be an instrument of meaning to the world about him in addition to letting the world have meaning for him. This well may mark the distinction between Oriental and Occidental civilization or, as Jung points out,[21] it may indicate the difference between the fundamental introversion of the Oriental society and the extroversion of Western society. To be sure, introversion carries with it its own methods of expression, but extroversion is less subtle and more unfettered.

It would be very easy to say that the most important of all our means of expression is language. Indeed, in this world of mass speech, both written and spoken, and the existence of vast educational and social structures that are dependent upon it, it well may be that this is mainly true. However, again we do not take into account the fact that man needs to function *in toto*. Our speech is important to us. We attempt repeatedly to impress the meanings of our lives on others by the use of language. It seems to make up for our lack of certainty or our inability to reason and think clearly. Yet in the final analysis there is always something to betray our language, and if our language can be betrayed and overshadowed by more important data of our personality, the question must be raised as to whether speech is really the most important of our expressive mechanisms.

There are many varieties of nonverbal language, ranging from writing, art, and sculpture to the expressive movements of the body. It is these latter which are our particular concern. Our reflex motions, gestures, posture, muscle movement, facial expression, and appearance are examples of the type of language which both precedes (preverbal) and supports (subverbal) spoken language. That it is impossible to overstate the importance of nonverbal communication is shown by clowns, comedians, and the masters of pantomime who can display with uncanny accuracy every emotion known to man without uttering a word.[22]

The one characteristic that can overshadow all the languages used is what might be called " the bearing of human presence." It is what Paul calls the " bearing about in the body the death and resurrection of Jesus Christ." Probably here is as good a time as any to make a proposition that seems to be fundamental in the witnessing to the truth of God in Jesus Christ, and that is that it proceeds most effectively in a " one-to-one " relationship. Granting that we can touch people and even help them through large groups in which our knowledge of our belief systems is demonstrated and reinforced, it still remains that if the gospel of Christ is essentially one of love, care, and concern for those about us, the only way in which ultimately we shall make the impact of this gospel upon others is in the normal conversation of a few, wherein at least one bears within himself the good news. Jesus' promise that " where two or three are gathered in my name, there am I in the midst of them " is probably less a rationalization for poor worship attendance than a recognition that intimacy and close sharing of life are important to the coming of God's Spirit among people.

Of course, all of us vary in the quality of the physical apparatus we use to answer the world. Not all of us are endowed with the best kind of physical equipment. Voices, physical features, size, temperament, and our general mien are given to us and they are not always to our liking. It is often difficult to keep this dissatisfaction from becoming a delimiting element in our responses. The Christian will come to understand that as his life develops he always takes on characteristics representative of the value structure of his religion. It little matters what our original equipment has been, for as we grow, mature, and become much more closely affiliated with the terms of the gospel, we subconsciously take on the very essence of this gospel which we cannot escape displaying in our response to the world. This is the first impression we make upon the world, for even if we do not speak, the language of the body is so important that words will come as an anticlimax. Dorothy Baruch has emphasized the importance of body love as an adjunct to good growth among tiny babies.[23] This is the sort of close affiliation of person with person that the Christian seeks to carry on; when we come into one another's presence the thing that speaks first and loudest is our personal bearing.

As significant as this trait might seem to be, it is nevertheless quite difficult to attain. It is highly personal, rooting back deeply into the personal devotion and reverence of the person who calls himself Christian. It is here where to be uniquely Christian will have its final effect, and our personal bearing will be trained. To speak correctly and even with refinement is almost a gift of the culture we live in. It is learned as we learn the manner of self-deportment. However, it is another matter to " learn " the art of " expression beyond expression," or the language beyond words. When mother instructs her young son, "Go kiss Aunt Jane and show her that you love her," the youngster will likely obey by doing the kissing, but showing the love is another matter. It can only be hoped for, not guaranteed.

Training for this type of language takes place in subtle ways. It is a process of growth wherein the faith, reverence, and love that we observe as we mature become a part of every sinew and movement of our lives. This is why in many instances the mere presence of someone else has been a help to us, for our lives have been most effective when we seem to have done only a little actual speaking. At the risk of oversimplifying the dynamics of the loving life, it is possible to say that sooner or later each person takes on the characteristic of a " yes " or a " no." That is, contrary to the usual assumption that life becomes more complex as we grow, the true pilgrimage of the individual should move from the complex to a more simple, straightforward, and honest expression of life. The Christian loses his sense of fear. He is not afraid to let himself be understood for what he is. He is aware of his shortcomings, and knows his abilities. He knows how to use them both, how to be abased and to abound, and soon this simplicity becomes a hallmark of his life, and one of the truly most significant aspects of his ability to communicate with other people.

To be sure, this type of language has many specifics of which speech is one, gesture another; and coupled with these are the many types of glances, grimaces, smiles, frowns, and other forms of expression that go to make up the things that people see upon us. All of these are employed when we act as persons. Some of us may be quite versatile and use all of them. Others may get along with the use of only a few. Some may be very much restricted in the way they employ their physical make-up to express themselves. Others may be quite free. Who of us does not know the person who can come into the room and immediately it seems as though his personality is pervading the whole scene? We also know people who may be in a group and yet be known to be there only by a very few, and maybe not even those near him. It is going to be quite useless for us to try to set down a list of techniques or suggestions whereby a person can perform his task as a Christian among other people. No type of teacher, witness, or preacher can be said to be more effective than any other type. But it is true that only in so far as we let our whole life become an expression of the love of God will our communication be worthy of the gospel we proclaim, "And we impart this in words not taught by human wisdom but taught by the Spirit" (I Cor. 2:13).

When we talk about human relations, we are talking about a great deal that is private as well as what is public. We see what goes on when people confront one another and when they function in small groups, but what must always be inferred is what goes on inside them in terms of the dynamics of their very private existence. We are able to detect when people are listening, and when groups of people have their eyes fixed upon some activity, we can reasonably assume they see what they are looking at. We hear people talk and take note of their gestures. All this overt behavior can be measured and evaluated. The decibel rating of the voice, its pitch and clarity, can be controlled to provide optimum expression. The hearer can be judged on the basis of quiet and eye focus, but what cannot so easily be understood is the way what is said and heard is organized inside the speaker and hearer. We sense our pleasure or displeasure with the way we act. We ask ourselves: "Why did I behave as I did?" "Why did I say that?" "Was it a good thing to say?" "Did I hurt someone?" "Did I help?", and in this way we perform an important service to ourselves by this "feedback" which gives us some idea of the way we are functioning.

This, plus the reaction we gain from others, is sufficient to tell us whether or not our means of communication is reaching the objective we have in mind. In fact, the rapidity of the give-and-take, plus the ambiguity of what is said and felt tends to cause us to generalize to the point where our feelings are "general," and we sometimes wonder why we feel the way we do. The privacy of these feelings makes them difficult to express to others. These feeling tones are based upon deep-lying psychological needs: the needs for satisfaction and gratification, the needs for assurance, the needs for the understanding that our relationships are valid and authentic, so that the organization of meaning becomes an exceedingly profound and compounded aspect of our lives. But it is precisely in this area the person must function as a Christian, for the Christian life touches the deepest-lying attitudes. It is more than sensing and expressing. It is more than telling and receiving. It is even more than discourse about itself. It is " the way, and the truth, and the life." It is the way things *are*, ultimately, with man. Man lives by being true to this way things are. It is this living which is organized in such a way so that all of life will be caught up in Christian encounter with the world.

The third dynamic, then, is that of organizing. Such organization is based first of all upon selection. From the masses of expression and stimuli of which we are daily a part, the Christian has to be selective, to know where to give his attention. All the sounds we hear and the sights we see have a hierarchy of meaning. To one person a bird may be just a bird, but to another it may be a special kind of bird, depending upon his interest in birds. For all of us, things are selected to be attended to as part of the normal life, but for everyone this selection is made on the level of values. We choose those things which are of greatest value to us, and upon which we have been nurtured. Every expression and all sensing we do in our world will fit somehow into this scheme of values that is predominant and dominating. The Christian cannot be unmoved by misery, or the slightest invitation to help. We will come to sense where we are most needed, and where our witness can be performed to the greatest advantage. After some practice of this discipline we shall establish an almost intuitive sensitivity to what is expected of us in all situations.

A second aspect of inner organization is a frame of mind appropriate to the situations we select. Those who study man are using the term " cognitive schema " to describe the way things are seen, and it applies both to the simple patterns wherein we perceive a thing to be a table, or to large patterns in which we view groups or classes of persons in a particular way, with prejudice, for instance. Gordon W. Allport has attempted to describe the sort of schema that would be normal for growing, mature persons.

> Now the style of life that welcomes rivalry within the constraints of potential inclusion is marked by a kind of *tentativeness*. It does not insist upon the absolute validity of its equations; it prefers a way of life without prescribing it for all; it possesses humor; it maintains its loyalties within an expanding and yet discriminating frame. Its judgments are tentative, its religion heuristic, its ultimate sentiment compassion. . . . It is the people with this outlook who in this period of rapid change give the world such stability as it possesses. Our problem is to increase their numbers.[24]

A most natural reservoir for such an increase should be the Christian community. It is here from childhood that we have learned that ultimate loyalty centers in the will of God and not in our prejudiced style of life. The Christian has learned that love is the dominating force in the life of the world, and must seek to bring his life into conformity with what we believe love to be. If love for ourselves, love for the things that will enhance our own lives, so dominate us that we are selfish persons, we shall structure our communication with others to preserve ourselves and to draw others into the support of our lives. If, on the other hand, our love is free to go out to others, we shall organize the things we hear in terms of providing for the benefit of others, the release of captives, the giving of sight to the blind, and the opening of doors to the imprisoned. Life will be organized for completely different purposes: such purposes as are in harmony with the will of God.

The Significance of Meaning

The end result of sensing, responding, and organizing is meaning, the fourth dynamic for communication. Things mean something to us, no matter who we are or what we do. This meaning is arrived at through the process of organizing the many expressions and stimuli of which we are a part. These meanings are both specific and diffused. They are specific because they impinge upon certain people. There are some people with whom we cannot easily affiliate. This may be due to experiences lying deep in our histories, but it is nonetheless true that some people wear better at a distance. With others we have no such difficulty. They mean comfort and friendliness and we seek out their association. How strange it is, then, that the command of the Christian is that he should go into all the world! And it is precisely at this point where so often we make things difficult for ourselves. If man tries to disregard the meanings that the world holds for him, he will find himself engaged in insignificant and unproductive relationships with people. If the teacher in the church school is not aware of the fact that a group of pupils will not all have the same meaning for him as an individual, he is doomed to failure. To become all things to all men is a difficult stage of relationship to reach, for "all things" in ourselves are apt to be exceedingly relative.

We bring, therefore, to every encounter a specific kind of meaning. We can feel it. It is not foreign to us. We know readily whether we feel comfortable with someone, or whether it is going to be difficult for us to establish rapport. Sensing this will tell us how far back we must begin in our Christian witness. And we must even face the probability that with some people our witness will hardly ever be effective. This is because the meanings of specifics which have grown up in our lives are going to inhibit us in our relationship with them.

It should not, however, be disconcerting to us to know that we are not competent missionaries to everyone nor able to teach equally effectively in all cases. This is probably one of the reasons why Jesus did not impress upon his disciples the technique of persisting with a person until he was willing to hear. Jesus was much rather willing to have them wipe their feet, turn aside, and go elsewhere, not only because of the hardness of some people's hearts but also because of the inability of all persons to speak in the name of Christ to others with the same degree of effectiveness. Moreover, our movements in the direction of others will be determined by general meanings which we have about our world. To be fearful, cautious, reckless, highly expressive, withdrawn — all these are features of man's personality which arise out of the meanings we give to life. Therefore we shall approach everyone with these as well as with the specific meanings that we give to our encounter with any given person.

It is this world view that dominates us. It grows with us and sooner or later becomes the true self that we present to the world; and it is out of this self and its view of the world that we speak. When we reach this core of meaning, we now have the very basis for all the listening and expressing we do in communicating the gospel. In fact, it might be said that it is neither the words nor the listening, but the meaning we bring to every situation which in the final analysis is the essence of communicating the gospel. Another way of saying " the Christian as communicator " would be to say, " the Christian as meaning." It is this meaning which is brought to bear in every situation. We can scare people off with our words only if the meanings they convey are either not understood or are so far removed from the words themselves that it is impossible to understand them. The church must stand judgment on both counts. Its meanings have been obscured by a too rich diet of traditional vocabulary, which shields its meanings. Von Bismarck says:

> It is the peculiarity of the word of God that passes through the Christian that it is not only word but action. That is why we as Christians are called upon to dispense happily with any Christian vocabulary, that the tradition of the church, and in particular its ghetto temptations, keep on hanging about us like an old coat we have inherited in order to live as men and women in the world with our brethren, and pray to God in this reality. Such true life will also find expression in our speech and has its own garment of language constantly renewed. We shall tell forth God's word in our own way, having regard to God and with our eyes on our neigh-

> bors. There is no recipe telling us how, but there is a promise, not only when Christians come to judgment but always for all time the words hold good for them in their responsibility to the world. " Take no thought how or what ye shall speak: for it shall be given you in that same hour what ye shall speak. For it is not ye that speak, but the Spirit of your Father which speaketh in you." (Matt. 10:19-20.) [25]

Two dangers continuously stand in the way of vital and clear expression of Christian meaning in our lives. First, the terminology used to describe the meanings is often too elaborate for the Christian. They are multisyllable words that somehow do not easily get to the level of meaning for those who speak them and consequently to those who hear them. It may be hopeless to expect that we shall find words to express adequately what our dogma has brought us to believe is essential. It may be there are no simple words for " regeneration," " justification," " sanctification," and other concepts in traditional Christianity which are so important to us. And it may not be wise for us to look for the simplification of these terms. Indeed there is a large place for professionalism within the Christian tradition where terms are constantly being refined and their meanings brought to light, but in the final analysis if these terms shield us from the meanings that lie behind them, our witness to the world will be as sounding brass and a clanging cymbal. This confusion of noise will prevent the meanings from coming through.

The term " theologian " should have meaning at another significant level – a level on which all Christians are involved. It has been customary to think of the theologian as the professional. He is the one who establishes the dogma, he pores over it, he lives with it, scrutinizes it, employs all elements of logic and metaphysics to refine it and keep it alive. But at another level he takes his place with the totality of humanity where everyone has the responsibility for becoming a theologian in terms of meaning. If there is one thing that Christianity has taught the world, it is that somehow all of meaning can be reduced within the framework of human life – any human life.

Its message is not only one of preconceptions *about* God, but certainly the interpretation and incorporation of God within the behavior patterns of human life, and to this degree everyone is able to participate. While some may express it in a more refined discipline of what they feel about God, others will express it in terms of daily lives where they become plumbers, accountants, electricians, and teachers. But at the very core of the lives of all these people there is a meaning that is made to no avail if shielded by the verbiage of the church.

A second danger is that the meanings of our Christian religion will be too far removed from the words we speak about them. The Christian community is slow to change. It is apt to express itself in terms that long since have lost their meaning, and in the process of enculturation this can become a truly delimiting factor. The transition from the things we do on Sunday morning to the things we do during the week is difficult. To be sure, both experiences are governed by some underlying basic concept of what religion is, but we cannot so divide our lives that what happens Sunday morning is unrelated to what happens the next day. However, it well may be that what happens when we leave this world of " secret " language to find that it does not fit the workaday world is that we withdraw altogether from talking to people about religion. Somehow, this must change. It has become necessary for us to speak, encourage, admonish, and simply to live among people as a loving person. In order to be ultimately effective love not only must carry with it our deep meanings but take on the kind of verbalization that will put these meanings into some form of adequate expression. It is to this end that the Christian is a communicator of the gospel.

Chapter III

" If I Speak in the Tongues of Men . . ."

Given these tremendous capacities for sensing and responding, and granting the existence of meanings in our lives which yearn for expression, it is inevitable that we shall do something about it. We will extend ourselves into the lives of other people. To withhold ourselves is difficult, and if we do so, it is only because the natural processes of moving toward others are frustrated. If carried to extreme, we become ill. To function normally man has to talk, gesture, look around, smell, and touch — to let his whole body be a part of the outgoing movement toward the environment. These capacities are somehow related to the fact that Christianity is a religion of extension. If the Christian gospel is designed to cover the entire range of human behavior and need, it is only natural that these needs to extend, and this natural propensity to communicate, must fall under its demands. Among other things Christianity gives meaning to the process of extension and provides a content that runs along it. Christianity is not a witnessing religion simply because this is a " new " way of God, or because it picks up this unique capacity in its development in history. It is a witnessing religion primarily because man is a witnessing creature, and to fulfill all of man's personality he needs a religion that can be carried into the world.

If theology is so difficult that the average person has trouble finding his way around in it, it is also true that just talking to one another is not quite so simple as it seems. We may have considered this the last stronghold of simplicity in a complex world. We may have felt that when life becomes too confounded for us, we can slip off and chat with a friend or neighbor. Little do we realize that what we are doing is so tremendously complex that experts in the field of communication have sprung up with a vocabulary just as baffling as the vocabulary of the theologian. Almost everyone thought he knew how to talk, see, and hear, but today, even in the church, classes are being held in human relations, group processes, and the skills of visitation, solicitation, and other forms of public confrontation. A church school teacher no longer stands up and simply delivers himself of the things he has absorbed through study during the week. He is now bound by a great many "trade secrets." He must know the dynamics of human behavior, understand how groups function, know his place as a teacher, know when to speak, when to be quiet, when to stand apart from the group, when to get into the group, how to "get people involved" (or uninvolved!), and a host of other complicating mechanisms, which, by the time he gets ready to "speak for God," are subject to the scrutiny of the specialist who wants to help him.

It will take more than the specialist to quiet us down, but his intrusion into our lives should not blind us to our obligation to ask ourselves how we should speak for God, and look at some of the simple qualities required for the normal interrelationship of people. There is probably a great deal of truth in the fact that we would be a lot less concerned about *how* we approach people if the meanings of our life were in true perspective. There is good Scriptural support (Matt. 10:19) for the assumption that if a person has a firm Christian grounding in his own life, he will automatically know what to say and when to say it. Jesus told his disciples not to concern themselves too much with what and how they should speak; for in the time that they were called upon to speak, the Spirit of the Lord would guide them. However true this ultimately may be, it is even more true that the dynamics of our interpersonal relationships are not quite so simple. If the meanings of our lives motivate expression and movement among people, it is also true that our expressions among people result in the changing, modifying, and intensifying of the meaning. This reciprocal process develops our areas of meaning by speaking out of those meanings, but those meanings are in turn developed by the way in which one speaks and listens; by the way one uses these facilities for human relations.

The Language of the Body

Where do we begin? Long before we are able to use words, our body uses a language all its own. It is only reluctantly and after a relatively long period of time that the language of the body is replaced by the language of the mouth. When Paul speaks, therefore, about " the tongues of men and of angels," he should be understood as referring to the total range of human output. We speak in hundreds of ways and it well may be that some of the senses that we do not normally associate with expressive behavior are in themselves expression and we should consider them as such. It is quite likely that the first thing to speak for us is our body itself.

René Spitz [26] has been interested in the development of bodily behavior in children. He has made experiments on children at one very strategic area, and that is to watch the development of the " yes " and " no " movements of the child. At a very early age, says Spitz, the child exhibits bodily movement indicating whether he is affirming or rejecting his environment. The negative movement is indicated by the rather inelegant term of " head rolling," or the sharp movement of the head from side to side. It is a rejecting act, indicating displeasure with something in the environment or maybe with the entire environment itself. It is an attempt to ward off annoyances, an endeavor to shake loose what is so uncomfortable and threatening. On the other hand, the child demonstrates what Spitz calls a " rooting behavior." This is an assentive motion, seen most clearly when the child is feeding at his mother's breast or a bottle. He moves his head up and down, "rooting" much like a little animal. This is a movement of assent, affirmation, and agreement with his environment. Things are good. He is "yessing." It is good to be here and he does not wish to be anyplace else. He does not particularly wish for anything to be moved out of the environment. He tolerates it, wants it, and accepts it as it is.

What is happening in these early years is the evolvement of one of the most fundamental "speech patterns" that man will ever possess, the ability in any situation either to affirm or negate his being where he is. Little argument should be needed to show how important this is for witness to the Christian truth. By the simple use of the yes and no, he may be saying more than we realize for the gospel. Indeed this may be exactly what Jesus meant when he said, "Let what you say be simply 'Yes' or 'No.'" The "yes" and "no" are primary, the *sine qua non* of human interchange. Any words beyond them are only an amplification of either of them.

Sometimes in the presence of others we are uncomfortable, do not want to be there, and have feelings of dislike for people around us, or even for the place we happen to be. It almost goes without saying that having these feelings, in some way or another we show them, if not immediately, sooner or later by the more complicated means of speech and actions. On the other hand, our behavior will conform to the feelings we have in situations where we feel wanted, comfortable, and in agreement with what is going on. The comfort or discomfort of being in the presence of another is the first act of speaking. This applies to the minister in the pulpit, the teacher before his class, or the person who is speaking to another on the street corner. I suppose many ministers have to face the fact that on some Sundays when they have to speak for God, they just do not feel like it. On the other hand, there are some Sunday mornings when they feel eager to speak. In either case what is carried by the voice somehow reflects what is carried within the basic "yes" and "no" meanings of each individual's life. Similarly, it would be ridiculous to assume that every church school teacher every Sunday morning jumps out of bed, claps his hands, and exclaims, " Oh, how wonderful it is to get up and teach my class this morning! " Life just isn't this way. No doubt, there are a great many Sundays when some teachers would rather stay at home, and all morning are bothered by a negative attitude toward what they are doing. We do not always feel good about the people we meet, or always enter our more intimate relationships feeling happy, contented, and in agreement. Things that happen to us make us feel disagreeable with anyone regardless of how friendly we have been heretofore. On the other hand, the very opposite may be true for all of these people. There may be times when the world seems good because we are happy, and to move into our relationships with happiness almost certainly guarantees a successful encounter with another person or group.

How closely related to the fundamental truth of God's word this is we can never know. Indeed, one might almost reduce the concept of the gospel to two terms, " acceptance " or " rejection." Knowing God to be a truly accepting person, we want to be like him, but knowing ourselves as we do, we know that we are capable of both kinds of behavior. Both accepting and rejecting can occur in the same experience, but here we stand with this " yes, yes," and " no, no," within the range of our capacity, and with them we move ourselves in continuous involvement with others.

Listening as the First Attentive Gesture

As was said earlier, these basic meanings and attitudes of being attentive will almost certainly govern our opening gestures in the presence of other people. The first gesture is to listen. Christianity has not always recognized as important this aspect of its witness. It is generally assumed that to communicate is to speak, to " spread the *word,*" and the Bible reinforces this by constant reference to teaching, preaching, prophesying, declaring, and exhorting, all having strong overtones of verbal expression.

We are active beings, and it is customary for us almost automatically to reduce our impulses to words. Even before the words appear, however, something more important happens. Our very presence in a situation says something before we have the chance to use words. To make good use of this preverbal activity is a highly developed art, the capacity for which in some people seems to be lacking. For all of us it is difficult. Usually we look for an opening into the conversation, displaying our eagerness to become involved, and seldom regard ourselves as an " opening " for other persons. The Christian's first impulse is invitational rather than aggressive. We must be attentive and learn how to listen and to be sensitive to the demands of the moment and to the dimensions of the particular confrontation. It may be in this first gesture that an entire relationship will be won or lost.

We listen not only with our ears but with our eyes. The ear, of course, is the primary listening post of the body. It catches the sound of anxiety or concern, of casualness or rigidity, the crisp tones of resentment or the easy tones of friendliness. It can tell when someone wants to " bend our ear " to unburden himself, or when someone is in a hurry, and does not need us under present circumstances.

However, in almost all normal interpersonal contacts, the eyes function before the ears. While our ears are listening for other voices, our eyes are already doing their own " listening." Nearly everyone has had the experience of talking to someone who was glancing around the room, probably trying to find someone more important to talk to. Or what minister, greeting his congregation following a service, has not been embarrassed to find himself shaking the hand of one person while talking to another? The church school teacher is constantly under pressure to shift attention so rapidly he cannot always center upon a single individual. Whether divided attention results from the fast-moving circumstances in which we find ourselves, or is the way we deliberately handle our close associations, it obviously cannot be invitational.

Being a " look-around " animal rather than a " smell-around " or even " hear-around " animal, our glances can take in the whole situation, and if we are sensitive to people's actions, it is not long before we have sized up the situation in which we are involved. Our glances invite affiliation and almost immediately indicate to another the level of our readiness for conversation. Our glance indicates " yes " or " no " to the degree that no other gesture of our bodies can do. Of course we can beckon with our arm or our hand, but this is subsidiary to the first beckoning of our glance. Couple this with the capacity to listen and we have here one of the most important facilities for " speaking with the tongues of men and of angels." We often know immediately through both looking and listening the level of needs of the people we are dealing with. Even in a large group we can sense the readiness of people. The church school teacher particularly, through a few moments' inquiry with ear and eye, can detect how ready the students are to respond to the situations. And certainly this is more than possible when we engage in a one-to-one relationship.

The Levels of Listening

First of all, it is possible to be attentive in an *absentee* way. The people are real enough and we are standing in the presence of their words, but we are not hearing them. Our minds are elsewhere. We feel we need to be polite and even try to force an external semblance of politeness, but we are really not polite at all. We are simply not there. Our first energies are being spent in maintaining a false pretense. In this kind of situation, conversation can proceed only a slight distance, and any attempt to think in terms of communicating the gospel of Christ is unthinkable.

A second level of attentiveness occurs when elements in the situation tend to *disturb* the focus upon the other one. He is speaking but we are listening with our attention divided by noise, interruption, or the transitory nature of the event.

A third level of attentiveness is *negative.* A surprising number of subjects can create contradictory feelings. Everything from local to world-wide issues will put people on different sides, in different political parties, or in different religious groups. While it may be true that there are two sides to everything, it is even more true that nearly every subject will find people divided on two sides regarding it, no matter where the truth happens to lie. In fact, some persons seem to react intuitively with negative feelings and expressions in all their interpersonal encounter. Such people do not listen; they spar. They engage in combat rather than encounter. This can even be expressed through bodily gestures such as ramming hands into pockets, covering the eyes, or holding back and even withdrawing physically from the situation. Eventually, the verbal responses will verify this negation no matter how gallant an effort is made to be positive and agreeable. Jesus recognized this when he said that agreeing with an accuser even on the way to court is a very important adjunct to communication.

At the fourth level of attentiveness, we are willing to listen but only in anticipation of the other person's finishing what he is saying. There is politeness in this behavior. Very likely this characterizes more of our conversation than any other level of attentiveness. We do not feel negative, nor absent from the situation. We enjoy the give-and-take of relating to people in this way. We enjoy getting into what we call a discussion, but nothing really happens because we are like two mountain peaks, each displaying its own form and integrity, but with nothing apparently connecting them. Admittedly, this is an entertaining pastime, and it has even been formalized into panels and symposia, but no one is really changed very much, nor is this expected to happen. We have come to believe that if everyone has the opportunity to express himself somehow or other the level of personality will be raised. This is questionable. Certainly if we believe that people must function in a "field of force" in order to accomplish relationships at their highest level, we must seriously question how much our debating and argumentativeness will produce effects worthy of the Kingdom.

Listening as Invitational

There is only one justifiable way that the Christian can come into the presence of other people. He will learn how to listen and listen completely. It should be emphasized again that this is difficult for many to accomplish. Our verbal expressions are such excellent defenses that to withdraw them makes us feel vulnerable. To get in our side of the picture is not only self-verifying, but we feel verified in the minds of others. Listening, therefore, can be threatening. We are not sure of the demands it will bring, nor what we shall do with the demands that do come. To listen is to have our souls open to attack.

Here is one of the reasons why the Christian religion and Western civilization generally are highly verbal. Christianity has something to defend. Its dogma is symbolized in words, and words are both written and spoken to interpret, explain, and verify the words. Every Sunday billions of such words are uttered on behalf of the faith. It would be interesting to know what proportion of those words are uttered in some sort of "defense" and how many are offered as a true testimony to the Spirit of God in human life. The words of Christianity, necessary though they be, are all symbolic of the "Word made *flesh*," a way of life, a condition of the human-divine being. This needs verification through sacrifice and love, both of which are expressed through the inviting and attentive spirit. Carl R. Rogers [27] has done us a great service in bringing us back to the fact that somehow or other the process of interpersonal relationship is carried on much more satisfactorily when at least one person in the situation is willing to be attentive and let himself be involved in the process of listening with his whole being. Speaking of an interview situation in which the counselor listens and invites the client to express honest feelings, Rogers says:

> The safety of the relationship with the counselor, the complex absence of any threat, which permits honesty even in the expression of inconsistency, appears to make this exploration

> very much different from ordinary conversation. One client explains that she has talked over all these troubles with her friends, yet in actuality hasn't done so. "I was really saying the thing next to the thing that was really bothering me." [28]

Such capacities are not reserved for the professional counselor. If Christians are to witness, they cannot be satisfied to deal with the " thing next to the thing." The attitude of invitation and bidding will welcome the entire person into the encounter. Since listening is so difficult, most of us think we do well simply to hold our tongues. This type of withdrawal is not enough. To be sure, holding one's tongue might be the thing to do in many instances, but accomplishing this usually requires so much energy that we fail to move on to the next step, and that is to truly invite people into our lives and establish the encounter at the level of feeling and, eventually, of meaning.

It is necessary, therefore, to put a loving act at the very beginning of our relationship with other people. It is mostly nonverbal; the other one senses it with his eyes rather than with his ears. He sees we are relaxed and not poised to oppose him. He sees we are a " soft answer " before he hears a word. He is accepted and invited. All of us have been in relationship where someone has an ax to grind. Very verbal, one defends his position with all he is worth. The other person accepts him, remaining relaxed and poised. The first feels attended to; a sympathetic thrust is made in his direction. Almost immediately, and in an uncanny way, this person shifts the focus of his bitterness, or at least softens it. He may even say such things as, " Well, I get pretty excited about this," or, " I guess you can understand the way I must feel about this." And from that point on the relationship moves to a deeper level. He knows he does not need to defend himself against the other, for the other has not felt it necessary to defend himself. This is true attentiveness. This is more than simply standing in the presence of another while he is talking.

The minister and church school teacher know well how difficult it is to understand this procedure, let alone incorporate it into their method. The training program for the performance of the professional services of the church has generally given little place for such technique. To be sure, with the rise of counseling and the resurgence of interest in shepherding people, we have entered an era where the minister, teacher, and chaplain have a greater opportunity to develop the art of being attentive. This augurs well for a new day, for the Christian has a right to speak only if he has listened.

However, the minister cannot tap the feelings of an entire congregation in a few moments, nor can the teacher walk into a church school class and " hear " immediately the needs of the group. He has enough difficulty establishing rapport after a week of separation, let alone being attentive and " taking a sounding " on the level of interest and readiness. Moreover, proficiency in this skill develops as an art, the performance of which depends upon long and deep association with the persons with whom we interact at the level of spiritual development. This means that an evaluation will be needed of the teaching of the gospel in our educational enterprise. It will mean, of course, that the teacher needs to couple this listening-seeing process with the verbal process. The way the teacher moves about, the way he confronts people, the way he demonstrates his feeling of " at-homeness," the way in which he directs his attention to the individual or group as these are needed, his ability to shut out all of the interfering data of the environment and focus directly upon one pupil when the attention demands it will gradually build up reciprocity of these two kinds of movement of the teacher in the group.

Guidelines to Listening

How is this listening accomplished? Although this book is not designed to be a primer on techniques, a few suggestions here might help illustrate this very important aspect of communicating the gospel. First, regardless of how ready or unready we feel to give attention to another, the Christian will invest his first energy trying to bring it about. The "professing" Christian is a "professional." He works hard at the thing he is supposed to do, whether he feels like it or not. Halford Luccock has described this attitude in his column in *The Christian Century.*

> One of the best definitions of a professional is "a person who can do a good job when he doesn't feel like it." He has learned his stuff. That definition fits the surgeons who can see twenty people in the office in the morning and then do five operations in the afternoon. When the fifth operation comes up at five thirty, does such a surgeon say with glee: "Goody, goody! Time for one more before dinner?" Not if he is in his right mind! He merely does it. And does it well. That surgeon is a professional.[29]

Human nature is capable of this. We cannot appeal to human weakness or even to repeated failure. We are developing a discipline, an art. And art is achieved only as the discipline is assumed; this is the method by which we learn to reduce the need for defense and thereby enhance our skills of invitation. Time and again we may have to call our attention back from its wandering. We may have to bring under control our feelings of negation when we hear people say things that run counter to our feelings of the moment, or what our Christian convictions happen to be. We should be prepared to accept anything that is said, no matter how contrary it seems to the very thing we are trying to profess. We must be ready to hear things said about God, the church, and other people that would not be said within the community of the redeemed. In our approach to the world we are not within the community of the redeemed. We stand alone with only God's love to accept feelings of hostility, resentment, criticism, and even slander. This will take considerable doing, and if we are accustomed to acting within a psychological framework that seeks for human adjustment rather than spiritual encounter, we will obviously withdraw from the attack, or attempt to meet it with a stronger attack. On the other hand, if we not only see ourselves as possessing a truth about God, but also see in this truth our responsibility for being permissive, accepting people, this "professing" will assist us eventually to function with people in a way that will bid them enter our lives and find there the event and spirit that have drawn them to us.

The second aspect of this spirit of attentiveness is that of getting below the content of what is being said to the level of what is being felt. Expressed behavior carries with it a weight of meaning. There is a reservoir of emotional information out of which all our expressions come. What is this feeling? What fears, doubts, and anxieties are being expressed? What questions are being asked? These will not always be seen readily. People are not free to talk immediately about the things that mean most to them. They need time. They need to have the assurance that when they speak they will not be hurt. They need to know that their true feeling will be accepted and respected by the person listening to them. Their words are simply vehicles for these deeper meanings and if we are to teach, preach, or otherwise communicate God's truth, we will set up no barriers to the deep meanings searching for expression. It is difficult to tell another how to be sensitive to feeling. This, too, is a by-product of the development of the art of communication. There are no agreed-upon ground rules for this game. It is somehow intuited after many experiences in which we have listened to people and seen through their words to the meanings of their lives. For the Christian educator, the question should be raised as to whether one year is long enough for a teacher to be associated with a child in his spiritual growth. Is not this too short a time to ensure a teacher-pupil engagement at the level of meaning?

The third thing to be done if we are to become adequate listeners and attentive to the needs and lives of others is to learn their language. Even though we live within a society that uses generally the same language, our own language is very private. The meanings we give to words are strictly our own and even though our language is such that we begin the process of communication easily, the symbol is never fully expressed by the word, for every person develops his own set of symbols. In many instances, both in people and in words, the symbols may turn out to be quite similar, but in other instances they are quite dissimilar. The word "mother," for instance, symbolizes something special to almost every person. It varies in degrees from hatred and rejection through sentimentality to mature love.

This is true also in the words of the Christian faith. Such words as "salvation," "regeneration," "church," "gospel," "cross," "Jesus," all carry highly symbolic meaning. Not only do these symbols vary according to denominational and theological belief, but even within the most cohesive and homogeneous groups, individuals carry their own private interpretation of their meanings. Even people outside the church have some image of what these terms mean, for in our society nearly everyone is born within earshot of the word "God," and "eyeshot" of the church. None of us can escape arriving at some meaning and interpretation of Christianity. This implicitly argues for the maintenance of the kind of relationship among people which will permit one to learn the symbolic language of the other. We can easily develop a global concept of our witness, and become almost indiscriminate in "speaking for God." We may even buttonhole people at unsuspecting places to talk to them about their soul. We should probably look at some reasons for this. We may take literally the statement of Jesus to "go into all the world" and take it in such a way that there are no limits, no logic, and no reason about where we settle down with our witness.

It may also be true that it is easier for some of us to talk to "the world" than it is to talk to those who are within the immediate arena of our experience. It is no secret that sometimes people who live closest to one another are the very ones who have the most difficulty communicating at the deepest levels. The stranger is safe. He does not know us well enough to see what is behind our word symbols, and it is easy to defend ourselves against him. People are always conscious of the boundaries of their spheres of activity. Persons close to one another come to respect these boundaries, and the best guarantee of being let alone is to refrain from bothering the life style of the other. Therefore, we may find ourselves going out into the world of people where encounter needs to occur only on the level of words. Admittedly, this may produce results. But if the development of a good testimony among people has anything to do with the knowledge of the meanings that lie below the symbols, then it seems only logical that the best place for us to be witnesses is among those with whom we have the deepest relationship; or when we go into the world, be patient enough to learn the inner language of the other. Only then can love do its work.

The Value of Speech

In the field of human relations, it has been assumed that people should refrain from talking as much as possible when they are trying to help someone. However true this may be, it is not because speaking itself is necessarily evil. Even though speech is for all of us to some degree a means of self-defense or a means of dominating the environment, this does not mean that speech in itself is wrong. In fact, it is one of the most important human assets. Sound is one of the most important powers man has discovered. It is not without some reason that the speech of man has been compared with thunder, or sounds of rushing wind, or the billows against the sea wall. People like to be impressed by the sounds of other people and by noise of almost any kind. We like to make sounds, even when no one is around to listen to us. We make sounds just to keep ourselves company.

However important it is to draw someone into our lives through attentiveness, it can hardly be enough. People expect something from us and this is their right, for if being attentive is the first requirement of Christian communication, being expressive runs a close second. Words are not wrong; speech is not wrong. Speech, just as listening, becomes wrong when it is used only as a means of protection and defense. Human language is a most extraordinary phenomenon, yet learning to speak is a natural and almost effortless process. Everyone, with only rare exception, learns to speak. It becomes almost a simple reflex like breathing and swallowing, and therefore sometimes divorced from all thought. In fact, words often precede thought, and we may even forget what we have said soon after we say it. Although all these shortcomings may be looked upon as a discredit to our speech, they are but a judgment upon our most important ally to our Christian witness, and to discuss communication without giving a great deal of attention to it would be futile.

One of the first things the Christian can do, therefore, is not to think of himself more highly than he ought to think just because he listens instead of speaks. There has come to be a subtle assumption among the professionals that if they learn how to listen they are somehow superior to the people who have learned how to speak, and that the good counselor does well when he is listening, and not so well when he is speaking. Nothing could be farther from the truth. People need to have us speak. It reassures them of their being listened to, of their knowing that they are at home with the person who is listening to them. Our speech carries the same kind of meaning that we expect the speech of the other to carry. It tells people what is underneath us, and although our attentiveness may assure people that we are inviting them into our lives, what our listening means will not be completely revealed until we begin to speak.

Sooner or later, if we speak long enough, people will discover what meanings our words convey. It has often been said that silence and verbal reserve indicate deep-running feeling and thought. This is questionable. It may just as well reveal stupidity, fear, or lack of understanding of what is going on in the environment. Communication will mean nothing unless we speak, and speaking develops exactly like listening, as an art and as a method of affiliation with the people in our life.

One of the first things that our speaking must do is bring into the open the meanings we believe the other is trying to convey. Do we understand him? Are we saying what he is saying? Are we catching the subtle overtones and symbols of his words? Carl Rogers has suggested that the next time we get into a heated discussion with someone in our family or group we experiment by asking each person to speak up for himself only after he has restated the ideas and feelings of the previous speaker. Probably little that we do could be more disarming either to the other person or to ourselves. We might even try to use his phrases, his terminology, his expressions, and when we come to terms that baffle him we ought to try to express the same sort of bafflement.

Our words are a kind of transition point in which the loose lines of meaning are being secured. They join the two persons in a common endeavor, but the juncture is precarious. The meanings are just being learned, so the words are cautious and tentative. Their purpose is to build a bridge and not simply to hurl ideas and symbols back and forth across a chasm. They help each person to understand that he is not involved in painful and conflicting competition. On the contrary, each person is free to enter the transition, knowing his meanings will not be immediately clear and willing to tolerate a period of clarification and explication. One of the most blessed achievements of our words, then, is that they state what the other person feels *in terms of ourselves.*

This is something more than mimicking or repeating words or even rephrasing the words of others. Words carry the communication event one step beyond understanding to the completion of the cycle, so that the person not only knows *that* we understand, but also *how.* Just as we expect the other one to be himself in our presence, so now we must accept the responsibility of being ourselves in his presence. We will not permanently succeed in deception. If, for instance, the words of the other one stir resentment in us, we must do something with it.

and to push it down or aside will risk its breaking out in uncontrolled expression. Our words can describe something of our feelings. "That hits me at a tender spot." "I guess I'm extra sensitive at that point." Our words, therefore, symbolize the meanings we gain, not only from the other person or from our own inner impulses, but from the total event.

It is at this point where the life of the Christian is always put to the test. To speak after the other one has expressed himself makes us very responsible. Upon this word, this phrase, this sentence, this little bit of the conversation rests the difference between the person's continuing in his quest for truth and life and his withdrawing from the scene. The importance attached to it might have something to do with the fact that we often resist assuming the responsibility. In fact, some concepts of human relations and counseling have suggested that our participation should only take the form of a "response" to the other one. If by "response" is meant the sort of reaction on our part which throws the burden of the event upon the other, then it is simply a way of escaping what is truly ourselves. If, on the other hand, the event is designed to make each person stand as an authetic being in the presence of the other, then we must accept the responsibility for being authentic. Harry Stack Sullivan has suggested that we communicate as "participant observers" and

> that we cannot make any sense of, for example, the motor movements of another person except on the basis of what we have experienced, done ourselves, or seen done under circumstances in which its purpose, its motivation, or at least the intentions behind it were communicated to us. Without this past background, the observer cannot deduce by sheer intellectual operations, the meaning of the staggering array of human acts.[30]

Moreover, we not only respond to what is said and meant by the other one but also to something that is wholly our own. We are responsible for adding something to the situation. To be sure, this is done within the dimensions laid down by the other one, but it may assume a different meaning, a new direction, a higher level of understanding, simply because of something that originates with us. We should not be ashamed of it. This is the lesson that is taught, and without a lesson there is no learning. Without the interposing of something that is truly ourselves upon the event we become a nonentity, an unclear voice. This is antithetical to *interpersonal* communication.

If we are willing to assume the responsibility for standing within the human encounter, we will come to learn that we have the power to modify it, for we actually change reality by our words. When we speak, something is thrown outward and anyone within reaching distance is hit by it. To be sure, some words we say do not change things very much, but other words may change them radically. Think of what may happen in a situation when the words, "I love you," or "I hate you," are used. Both of these phrases can push life in entirely different directions. Words can be of condemnation and judgment, praise and acceptance, or they can demonstrate a lack of understanding. They can create embarrassment and destroy a relationship or tie together things people have been talking about. All of us have had experience in which almost miraculously the tone of a conversation, class session, or meeting has been changed and new levels of understanding have been reached. It is precisely this that must occur when the Christian speaks. He must expect things to change and he must expect his contribution, being Christian, to change things for the better. To be sure, because of our lack of experience and ignorance of what ought to be said, we shall not always accomplish what we had hoped and we may even say things that will frustrate rather than enhance the Kingdom of God. This risk must be run as we develop the art of speaking. Any behavior involving assertive action has a target that, in spite of our intentions, is sometimes missed badly. To hit it with appropriate intensity requires discipline.

Here again we face the complications of the magic associated with our speech. Just as there are private meanings in the speech of the other one, our speech in turn carries our private meanings and these are usually supported by the private meanings of the groups to which we belong. If we speak for God among the people, we speak for him out of the context of the church. It is the church that sends us out, gives us the commission to go and teach. Even what they mean to us may not be exactly what they mean to other Christians within the church. Thus if two Christians talked to the same person, both symbols and meanings might be completely different. Sometimes our speech becomes almost a magical formula to be tacked onto our conversation at convenient points, to carry the weight of belief and feeling that we fear will not be carried in any other way.

Such magic comes dangerously close to superstition. Is there any fundamental difference between the person who says, "God bless you" when another sneezes, and the person who habitually (and unthinkingly) says, "God willing" after many statements of purpose and planning? Add to this the countless numbers of phrases that have become the private property of the church, and therefore the private property of the individual, so that when he demonstrates them in his conversation with others he is employing symbols not easily communicated. In another chapter we shall explore the fundamental authority present in the relationship of communication; suffice it to say here that this authority cannot be found within the words used in the relationship regardless of the reverence they hold for us. As much as we may believe that the Christian community is held together by agreed-upon words, phrases, and dogma, we cannot infer that merely in these formulations we find our words for the world. In other words, our assertive behavior is governed by both the nature of the inner impellent, and the target it seeks. We must search for a different purpose in our conversation than simply to affirm the individual and group meanings, no matter how important they seem even to the Christian community that originates and nurtures them.

Six Purposes of Speech

What can words accomplish? What is their use in communicating the gospel? First of all, words should be interpreted as deeds. The distinction between saying and doing is mostly imagined. Saying *is* doing. It is the performance of an act, the doing of the deed, sometimes a more significant deed than we give it credit for being. Simply to say something in the presence of the other may be the very kind of work and deed that will accomplish the most good, and something that our manual activity could never accomplish. Who could for a moment suppose that the church school teacher is not " working " when he is engaged in verbal encounter with a class. Who can say that the minister in the pulpit is not performing a deed? They are deeds that stretch imagination, deepen the questions about life, purpose, and God. It is not simply for convenience' sake that most treatment for emotional disturbance takes place in a speech context. Words establish the base point from which we look at the past and govern subsequent action. To speak to people is to walk with them, share their burden, and accept their lives. No amount of activity can displace the need to perform the decisive act of saying, " I love you."

In fact, it might be said that this may be the hardest way to perform a deed. In time of need we can give food, shelter, or clothing, but who has not suffered the pain of not knowing what to say when another has suffered tragedy for which material aid is useless. It does not take a great deal of courage to go out of the way to help someone to his feet, but to speak the word that comes from our best selves to meet the need requires remarkable ingenuity. We may not speak it because we want to be sure that it will be accepted or appropriate. Since speech must satisfy many conditions – our feeling, the need of the other, and the community that teaches us how to speak – the deed of speech is performed only with difficulty. However, if we feel the readiness to speak, if we feel that all things have conspired so that what we must say is obvious, if we understand the chances of failure and of being misunderstood, by speaking in a "holy boldness" we perform a most excellent deed.

In the second place, speech is the shortest distance between our inner lives and the inner life of another. We have seen how this applies to others when we listen to them. The greatest compliment we can pay the other person is that our words are honest and do not hide the meanings underneath. It is no secret that between our words and the core of our lives there is a wide gulf fixed. Joseph Addison's essay "Frozen Speech," in *The Tattler* of November 23, 1710,[31] is a satire upon man's tendency to use language designed to cover up our true feelings and, as a by-product, confuse other people. The plot of the essay concerns a group of men who were marooned in a frigid climate. It became so cold they could not hear one another; the words froze before they got away from the men's mouths. Addison describes the phenomenon in this way:

> We soon observed that in talking to one another we had lost several of our words and could not hear one another above two yards distance . . . after much perplexity I found that our words froze in the air before they reached the ears of the person to whom they were spoken . . . the sounds no sooner took air than they were condensed and lost. It was now a miserable spectacle to see us nodding and gaping at one another, every man talking and no man heard.

Such an improbable condition is no more than a stone's throw from what actually happens in our speech. It does not take a frigid climate to make our words nothing but gaping at one another, everyone talking, no one hearing, not because our words are frozen but because what we talk about is not related to the emotional content of our lives, but is actually so much protective coloration to shield the very feelings we need to share.

Eventually, however, the meanings will emerge in spite of the words. In Addison's essay, when the thaw came:

> We now heard everything that had been spoken during the whole three weeks that had been silent. My reader will easily imagine how the whole crew was amazed to hear every man talking and see no one opening his mouth. We heard a volley of oaths and curses lasting for a long, long while and uttered in a very coarse voice, which I knew belonged to the boatswain, who was a very choleric fellow and had taken this opportunity of swearing at me when he thought I could not hear him.

And finally, Addison says:

> I must not omit the names of several beauties in Wopping which were heard every now and then. This betrayed several amours which had been concealed till that time, and furnished us with a great deal of mirth in our return to England.

If our words are used to conceal our beliefs, feelings, levels of meaning, and our true status before God, then without question our speech is wrong, very wrong, and all the suspicion that has been aroused concerning its validity is not without foundation. If, on the other hand, our speech becomes a vehicle to the reservoir of our own fund of emotional information, then it serves a purpose for which we need not be ashamed and which, even in those encounters where much listening is needed, will have some meaning in the relationship.

In the third place, our words, like listening, are invitational. If our words do not arise from our basic meanings, they must nonetheless be motivated by something. Unless we believe that all that is possible to religion and Christian experience is known by us, understood by us, and communicated by us, we will be in a position to think of our encounter with the other one as a quest for deeper meaning. No matter how certain the meanings, our words should aways permit the encounter to continue. The final, authoritative word will stop the encounter, or at best, veer it in another direction.

Jesus used words in exactly this way. In fact, the gospel writers focused upon his eyes, hands, and words, and the last are always in the form of a quest. His words invite others to think. Even when he forecasts the downfall of Jerusalem (Matt., ch. 24), the words "he who endures to the end will be saved" (Matt. 10:22) make the listener want to ask more questions about the ways of endurance. His injunction concerning taxpaying (Matt., ch. 22), whereby we render to God and Caesar their due, is a marvelous basic principle, but in reality it creates more problems than it solves. The hearer is invited. He must continue this quest, and even when Jesus moved away from the relationship, he left people continuing the encounter. They wondered at his sayings.

The other one helps us in our quest for meaning just as we are trying to help him. The questions he asks may be questions we have not asked ourselves. The terms he gives to his interpretation of the Christian religion may be the terms that we have not ourselves given to our own religion. The Christian will need to learn that his witness is not a one-way street. The church does not possess some sort of energizing force to be volunteered or withheld according to its whim. One overarching belief about God is that he works in the world at his pleasure and not at the pleasure of man. Therefore in conversation, search for meaning is a reciprocal activity as two people stand in the presence of the third. The way the minister invites the congregation into his own growth, the way the teacher lets the child express meanings that will help the teacher build his own life, are evidences of this kind of word usage.

There seems to be a great deal of difference between what we believe about this type of encounter and what we actually do about it. Almost generally it is admitted that the teacher learns more than the pupil, but it is not taken seriously enough to make it a point of discussion. The teacher is the essence of competence, at least, before his pupils. He holds a kind of prior place. He has the edge, so to speak, in this quest for life. To think of significant movement from pupil to teacher is to suggest failure or incompetence. Moreover, the Christian who communicates his faith may do so with the feeling that he can learn very little, especially from the sinner, that the sinner can teach only that which will negate the good, or at least threaten it. We can try to handle this by disassociating the sin from the sinner, but this is hard to do, and as a result we engage in the kind of conversation that does not search for meaning for ourselves, but rather draws meaning out of the other for his sake alone. No greater rebuke can be given to a person than the subtle implication that he can mean nothing to us. Therefore, our words are a search for meaning – meaning for the other one, for ourselves, and for the encounter.

Our words also are used to bring about change. Change must come from within the person. One's willingness to change is probably the best condition for change, but no matter how much change is wanted, it cannot be accomplished until the person himself accepts the responsibility for its occurrence. However, there are much more subtle implications for the meaning of change. In talking with people, especially about their spiritual growth, of course one important objective is to bring about change in the other one, but we are also seeking change in the encounter itself. In fact, it is only the *event* that our words can change, and it must be changed in such a way that all participants can feel free to change and grow. Every word brings some sort of modification into an encounter, and it is no longer the same after we have spoken it. However, we have not felt comfortable being " directive." The teacher and the preacher have both been taught in recent years to be very careful about being " authoritarian." Everyone disclaims anything having to do with authoritarianism, and we are very happy if we are considered democratic, simply because this means that we are not authoritarian. To be sure, to maintain a nonauthoritarian atmosphere in which people can function is highly desirable, and we have only to look around us to see what havoc authoritarian persons and groups can bring upon a society, or how an authoritarian person can utterly debilitate the life of another person.

Instead of starting with the term " authority," why not start with the term " strength "? At least this sounds a little more domesticated and not quite so threatening, and it much more closely characterizes the type of verbalization we are here describing. Speaking is an act of strength projected upon the world with purpose. If we were to deny this strength, we would deny speech altogether, for every word carries with it a measure of effectiveness in the encounter, and to this extent it brings change. The Christian does not use words that intrude upon the other person, but they certainly do intrude upon the event, make an offering, structure a new dimension, apply a new truth, clarify meaning, bring up from the reservoir of their own meaning another perspective, another way of handling the situation. Words can do this without cutting down the life of the other. It is only when our words are not directed toward the situation, but rather toward the other situation in intrusive ways that we can be accused of authoritarian tactics. To be sure, sometimes we stand within the event with such emotional investment that we must suffer the consequences of the change. But here again we must tolerate the patience of developing an art. This is not accomplished by applying rules and formulas, but rather by developing a sensitivity to the use of our words so that they broaden the base of encounter and invite meanings to emerge.

The fact that these words not only change, but create, provides a fifth purpose for the use of words in our relationships. Here again is something that is drawn from the basic understanding of the Christian faith. Words that create are symbolic of the creative act of God. One of the simplest things to do is to change. One of the most difficult things to do is to change in the right direction. Our words will always do one of these two things: they will cause the event to take on more difficult proportions; or they will cause it to move on in such a way that persons and meanings are drawn into a quest for the Christian life.

In the sixth place, our words are constantly serving the purpose of bringing people to the threshold of the predominant feeling tone of the situation. Beyond all the minor pulls and releases that occur when people relate to one another there is a dominant, overarching feeling tone that characterizes the situation. When we have gone home from church or from a meeting we say it was a good meeting or it was a bad meeting, not because of the sum and total of events, or because we have put events in the ledger or debit column and added them up to see which came out greater. We make our judgment rather on the basis of an over-all feeling we had about what went on. When we encounter another person, we like or dislike him not necessarily because of specific things, but rather because this whole encounter has developed a tone that is felt by the heart. Joost A. M. Merloo says:

> Would you convince your opponent? Then touch his heart – if he has one. One cannot conquer anyone's belief with words and arguments. He merely adjusts them to his own truths and prejudices – unless he likes you.[32]

Chapter IV

". . . And Have Not Love"

Attentiveness, speech, and gesture are symbols of an event. They cannot occur outside an event. Even the most casual expression implies a relationship deeper than the words themselves. A hurried greeting carries with it a great many overtones of relationship beyond the familiar terms. Everyday we have the experience of saying "hello," and then wondering whether we should stop to make more of the occasion. We are wondering what the "event" really is. Have we satisfied it by the "hello" or should it persist a little longer? Any human encounter is bound to find the participants maneuvering to determine the level and type of event in which, at the moment, they are willing to become involved. In all encounter we sense something trying to occur that is far more significant than all visible and verbal movement. In fact, it is the structuring of these events for which words are responsible. No matter how broad or suggestive our speech may be, it becomes a useless technique and tool if it does not succeed in structuring an *event* characterized by emotional interaction.

Picture two people meeting each other on the street. As they begin to speak, their words become embellished with all kinds of feeling tones. Uncertainty, joy, sadness, purpose, friendliness, and doubt begin to take over. They finally develop an image of each other and they are no longer just talking. They are building something between them that will prove to be either an impenetrable wall or an arena in which each of them can act freely. This may not be what is intended in the encounter, but it is precisely what happens. It cannot long maintain itself apart from value formations, for man seems to need to perform these spiritual deeds in the presence of his fellows.

The Problem of Love in Christian Communication

The problem of love has been dealt with at length in other works,[33] and while it does not constitute our primary consideration in this survey, it is nonetheless important that we give some attention to the part it plays in the act of communication. It certainly has something to do with Christian communication and probably we are discussing the most significant aspect of communication when we ask what it means to communicate "in love." Love is often defined as a noun, a kind of "condition" into which we ought to move, a climate in which things are right, good, happy, and joyous. It is thought of as a form of life one possesses, as we possess the economic or social structure from which we draw benefits. It may even be thought of as a construct or a particular framework in which people act and function, and in which all relationships are governed by some overarching law that dispels everything unlovely and wrong.

It would be more helpful for our purposes here if we looked at love as an active verb. Indeed, it might well be argued that there is no love apart from the loving act, that love is a condition not so much of being but of acting. It is the "way" of the human event that is loving only if the meanings, gestures, and words of the event are loving.

It should not be difficult to see, therefore, how the Christian reaches his highest and most meaningful performance when he engages in the act of loving, and introduces its dynamic into any situation. This is testimony and communication as a Christian act. This is the very frontier of the carrying of the gospel and wherever a Christian extends his life in terms of a loving act, it is then that the gospel of Christ is being proclaimed. To face the implications of this is a monumental task. Even to contemplate the minister in his pulpit, or the Sunday school teacher before a class of children, or neighbor's talking to neighbor, and then to make judgment about the degree of love that is present in any of these forms of communication, is a hopeless task. It is especially confounded by the fact that these loving gestures are in themselves so subtle, so refined, so hidden, that any analysis tends to cause them to dissolve.

Yet it can be taken for granted that man has the capacity to express and interpret everything he feels. It would be a serious loss if we were to love without being able to talk about it, or use words to indicate what love means to us and how it works in us. Moreover, we could hardly learn the art of loving unless somehow or other we were apprised of our failures and knew exactly where our words were carrying hostility in the guise of love, or whether love was present without one's recognizing it.

The Loving Act as a Human Event

How do we extend ourselves in loving ways? In the first place, the Christian will be conscious that his very entrance into any situation is contributing to the construction of an event, an incident filled with feeling. It may not be history-making or headline-creating, but an event it is nonetheless, and exceedingly important to the persons who are engaged in it. For one to enter the presence of others is to create an event of human interaction. However much we may take pride in being individual selves, our extension into the life of another makes it necessary to *define ourselves in terms of the event* we are in the act of creating. Whatever we say (or do not say) and whatever feeling tone is present will contribute to the construction of this event. What is a sermon but the minister's leading people into a number of events in the consideration with him of those things which he believes important enough to bring to their attention? What is the teaching of a church school lesson but the constant encounter of persons in events where learning and growth are possible to those involved in the process? The most casual conversation is but the movement of life along a series of encounters, each of which has its own meaning, each building upon the preceding one and contributing to the one just ahead, finally bringing to bear a particular kind of relationship that will change either or both persons.

The life of Jesus is to some degree distorted when we try to make it look like a totality or something that flows evenly from beginning to end. It was rather a series of events, the majority of which were encounters with others. The gospel writers were trying to impress the church with the fact that Jesus' love was manifest in a series of episodes in which the arena was open for the movement of life into loving ways. It would not be unprofitable to see our relationships in terms of episodes where person encounters person and where we can ask honestly whether or not our human encounters were events of love.

The meaning of life, therefore, is demonstrated in the single event, regardless of its size or importance. Each episode of human involvement is judged on its own merits, and cannot be lost in a " total picture " of life. To count up our liabilities and assets, weigh them against each other, and find we come out on the ledger side may be very gratifying, but we are still left with the question as to whether in the single encounter we have been able to structure an event that has for its meaning the acts of loving.

Love as Bearing

What are the characteristics of this event? How is this encounter carried on " in love "? In the thirteenth chapter of I Corinthians, Paul is answering this question by listing the attributes of love and finally indicating what it does in human relationships: it " bears all things, believes all things, hopes all things, endures all things."

These, like the love that they describe, cannot be defined apart from the persons participating in them. They are active verbs, and for our purposes the verse might read, " In all human events the Christian will be a bearing, believing, hoping, enduring person." They are conditions of personal encounter.

They are the episodic dimensions in any relationship whose purpose is in any way interpreted as a Christian witness. The first of these is *bearing,* which means much more than simply "putting up with." It is the willingness of one person to bear the responsibility of being involved in an interdependent relationship with another.

There seems to be something in the very origin and quality of all matter that requires interdependence. The single tree is in a far less favored condition than the trees that gather themselves together in a grove, or a forest, where each is able to offer some protection in terms of the other and in turn receive protection from those around it. Very few species of animals eagerly crave aloneness. Their desire to function in groups is something more than simply liking to have other animals around. There is an interdependence, even a division of labor, among them that ties up the life of each one with the lives of the others. People are not immune from this sort of relationship. Our very existence depends upon an intricate intertwining of our lives with the lives of countless other people. The simple business of food production and processing, for instance, makes it possible for us to live in a large group of people. Our work habits are conformed to "team work" and the signals we develop in order to carry on our interdependence constitute a fabulous network that makes us wonder why man should ever not find loving the easiest way of relating.

It is no secret, however, that in the very midst of this need for one another our essential relationships are characterized by almost a complete controversion of this process of interdepending. We vie with one another for status, position, and wealth. We seek to prove our goodness in one another's presence, or validate the goodness of those like us. That love and competition can exist together is almost unbelievable, but exist they do; and the Christian finds himself constantly breaking into a pattern of interpersonal struggle which is almost foreign to the thing he has to offer. He offers the only sane rationale for all types of interdependence, and for every situation in which people function together for the welfare of the other. He comes into the event with the desire to bear the responsibility for standing in the relationship, with only the expectancy that the event be characterized by love.

One of the most insightful analyses of the human condition is found in Erich Fromm's *The Sane Society*,[34] where he pictures man's existing in a state of embarrassment, torn between two forces that are constantly claiming his attention.

> Self-awareness, reason, and imagination disrupt the "harmony" which characterizes animal existence. Their emergence has made man into an anomaly, into the freak of the universe. He is part of nature, subject to her physical laws and unable to change them, yet he transcends the rest of nature. He is apart while being a part; he is homeless, yet chained to the home he shares with all creatures. Cast into this world at an accidental place and time, he is forced out of it, again accidentally. Being aware of himself, he realizes his powerlessness and the limitations of his existence.[35]

It is this very type of struggle in which the Christian himself is cast, the only difference being that he has somehow been able so to orient his life that he has not lost sight of or hold upon his eventual destiny. And this is precisely what he brings to others, albeit unfilled and probably even undeveloped.

Let us imagine a person in need of help at this very point. He wanders aimlessly through the events of his life, each of the episodes forcing him to defend and authenticate himself in the presence of others. He feels uncomfortable when others make their claims against him because he must reply in kind to show that his claims are just as valid. He does not quite understand the things for which he was made. All he can understand is that he is involved in the struggle at a very earthy level, the struggle for status, for security, for some sort of validation of himself as something a little higher than the animals. He even thinks of himself in animal terms, referring sadly to his being in a "rat" race and this in contradistinction to his being a part of the "human" race. Being unable to spring himself out of this earthly existence he must contrive to become a faster rat; thus his life is devoted to the pursuit of inhuman, unlovely goals.

Then one day he meets a Christian. At first the encounter is like all encounters. There is no reason to suppose this event will not proceed like all others – informal disregard for deep meaning and concern. But suddenly this event does not develop as expected. He is listened to and finds someone who, instead of trying to use him for his own ends, is interested in him. He finds himself gradually forgetting about the wall he must build about himself as his words are accepted by one who understands human weakness and uncertainty, and is not threatened by sharing it with another. This is a different world. It is as though something strange has happened, so strange that perhaps at first he isn't willing to accept it. It must be some sort of trick. It must be this year's " track " on which the " rat race " is run. To be sure, these things change from year to year and new techniques are developed whereby people enhance their own interests; certainly there must be some hidden angle!

A first meeting with the Christian does not change his approach to people, except that there has been a seed deeply planted in his thinking. It makes him just a little uneasy. He looks for signs of this same technique to appear in others, but when they do not, he forgets. Later he meets the Christian again, and is literally disarmed by attentiveness that invites him to talk about his true self. Instead of bantering opinions, he is caught up in a disposition of bearing. There is even more than the lift to self-esteem one gets when he is told he means something to the world, to the company, to the office, or to the church. He is suddenly aware that he has meaning beyond his " marketing value " to the world. In this encounter with a Christian he actually has value *as a person* to another person.

Probably the second time he cannot be fully convinced. He is too accustomed to the ways of his world. To find someone whose defenses are down and whose interests seem to run toward him rather than to the reinforcement of his own life seems incredible. However, he is not dealing with an impatient person, for in every conversation with this Christian there is something unfamiliar to the world he knows. There is not only the patience and understanding one can find in many people, but a genuine interest in sharing. The conversations move to a level of *inter*-participation and *inter*-depending, based upon a " oneness of condition " in which they stand. He finds himself seeking out the Christian because the event of their being together is not simply the construction of agreed-upon barricades from behind which they will hurl their own ego-gratifying ammunition, but rather, a table spread for an event of Christian love. It has arisen because one person was willing to bear the responsibility for himself, for another, and for a human encounter in which God's way was at work.

Love as Believing

The second attribute to which the Christian aspires in his relationship with this person is to accept him exactly as he is. By now this is an ancient interpretation of a good interpersonal relationship, but it carries with it some subtle implications we do not fully face. Christian people are prone to adhere to deep-seated clichés which persist in spite of constant reinterpretations. One of these has to do with the Christian's image of personality, not what personality is in theory, but what is actually seen in human encounter. Such clichés as " look for the best in people," or " look at them for what they can become," are familiar examples of acceptance, but do they mean the same as " believing all things "?

The " I-thou " relationship certainly has meaning in terms of the " thou." Does it accept only the best in the " thou," or is it willing to accept an unqualified " thou "? To accept persons at their best is to attach a penalty to life, and in a subtle way we insist upon high level of performance before acceptance is possible. To accept persons *in toto* may be difficult, but it certainly fits readily into the concept of love which Christianity promises and promotes, for Christianity is a way of " believing in " in addition to "believing about." The term "acceptance" has found favor in the Christian's vocabulary. However, it can stand for a wide range of attitude. For the most part, it carries with it the implication that "I will tolerate you," or "I will let you come into my life," and this can carry with it very wholesome and creative implications. It may even suggest that the one doing the accepting would be permissive enough to accept a person with all his faults. But to many persons such surrender of their own lives into the life of another is so threatening that subconsciously we harbor a "cut-off" point beyond which we cannot "believe in the other." We should understand, then, the nature of the arrangement of people in an event built upon love. What does it mean to "believe" in another?

For one thing, it is an attitude of "ultimate encouragement." At all costs it permits each of the persons to be completely himself. Whatever passes between two persons, it can never draw them so close together that they are ever robbed of their identity as persons. Let us look again at our man of the world and his encounter with the Christian. He has been disarmed by the strangeness of the relationship in which he finds himself. The interest another has taken in him now makes him interested in himself. He not only feels that another believes him, but the entire relationship becomes one of trust. He is baffled by his next involvements. Being encouraged by our Christian to show what kind of person he really is, he lets escape some things that are deep within him. He may even get around to confessing what he is and what his true impulses are, even to hostility or resentment, which now he feels he can display without someone's punishing him for it. These first displays of negative feeling may be accompanied only by further threat and disturbance, for speech is coming faster than thought. Even though in previous encounters he has met only acceptance and understanding, maybe his friend will not permit things that are less acceptable in him.

Indeed, the Christian might be tempted simply to reassure, and quickly terminate the self-exploration going on in the life of the other. However, he is not afraid that the expression of hostility will damage a relationship, and so he encourages the other to continue, knowing that even negative expression is no threat to the encounter. The Christian is not quick to gloss over, to give assurances, to offer unwarranted support, or to put the other at ease, for he has learned not only to believe the best about people, but to believe in people, good and ill. And the Christian does not hurry the other one over the rough spots, for among other things love is never in a hurry. This is what Paul means when he says it never ends. The event is charged with enough anxiety without adding compulsion.

In an unhurried way the person now has the opportunity to do what he could never actually do before. He can look at what he is in the presence of what the relationship is going to permit him to become. He does not compare himself with the Christian who is righteous, for making comparisons would force a retreat into his old ways. He cannot be made better by comparing himself with others, not even with the most righteous of persons. The Christian is not eager to "create" another in his own image. He sets an example, not of what the other one can become if he tries hard enough, but of full trust that where two or three meet in the name of Christ, something can happen to the lives of all participants.

It is only in this environment of "believing" that the person sees for himself the alternate possibilities within the framework of his own existence, and in the presence of this terrible encounter, the Christian stands by. He has calculatingly attempted to do nothing that would call attention to his own righteousness. He has done nothing that would impress upon the man that underneath he is deliberately trying to get the other to become as good as he is. He only knows that if given a chance all men will soon see themselves for what they are, however unpleasant it may be. But what a difference between looking at ourselves in a world where what we are causes so much pain that we cannot face ourselves, and seeing what we are in the presence of another who helps us see our embarrassment as a strength and not a weakness.

It is at this juncture in our acts of communication that Christianity in general and the Christian in particular has not done full justice to the meaning of the incarnation. Christians have always been rather certain about the office of Christ in the world. Although there may be some marked differences in the theological presuppositions about the incarnation and the ultimate sacrifice of Christ, it is realized by all that they represent some form of burden-bearing, and that what Christ accomplished on the cross has some relationship to the sins of the world. With the high degree of certainty about the concept there is a corresponding low degree of certainty about the Christian's interpretation of his own role in the act of redemption. If we are to be loving people, it then seems to stand to reason that even the ultimate meaning of the loving act falls within the domain of the Christian witness. The Christian has been somewhat reticent about seeing himself in such a Christ-like role. He does not readily warm up to the idea of being a burden bearer, let alone see himself in the role of sin bearer. Feeling that this has been accomplished by Christ on the cross, he suspects that little he can do will have any bearing upon or in any way resemble this one final act. If this be so, then we must admit to a serious gap in the process of Christian communication. If the incarnation cannot be understood as the very foundation of Christian communication, it can then only be reduced to a fetish, and its meaning veer off into misunderstood terminology in Christian dogma that will simply scare away anyone confronted by it.

Love as Enduring

In order to continue our discussion in the last paragraph, we will reverse the order of the last of Paul's characteristics of love. We will deal with the way in which love is enduring. It participates in the fundamental duress of life. It does not escape its responsibility for the constant renewal of its activity in the Christian's acts of communication. Not only does it identify and accept; it also endures. It not only bears the condition of the human encounter but also shares in the reconstruction of life within the event. The Christian then puts himself in the position where he can honestly say to the seeker in his presence: " Let your sin be mine as well. Let the stress you feel, the deep guilt and the horror that you feel for yourself, all be shared with me. Not only do I want to understand and accept, but somehow in this relationship I am part of your condition because I am part of this event." The Christian may not even sense this sharing as " taking over " the sin of the other. What it really means is that the Christian, be he ever so Christian, stands before God still under the judgment of sin. The hallmark of Christian maturity is not the employment of time in enumerating advances in righteousness ("not jealous or boastful; . . . not arrogant or rude "), but is found rather in a deepening involvement in the sin of human life. He is asked to endure something that might not be his own, but comes to him in the life of another.

To become so involved is to translate the redemptive act into the everyday acts of communication. Thus to close the gap between dogma and witness is the ultimate goal of the Christian as communicator. To let the fact of God's redemptive act in history appear only in our religious community as dogma is not sufficient, even if it is continuously redefined to meet the conditions of current thought. Until it is translated and literally transformed into a working principle by which the Christian confronts the world, it will be of little or no value, even as dogma.

By participating in this kind of communication the Christian in the truest and finest sense becomes a theologian. He may not qualify as a practitioner of the things *about* God, but he need make no apology for being a practitioner of the things *of* God. As a witness, he engages in the one form of interpretation that, above all other forms, will bring redemption to our society if carried on by enough people in enough places at enough times. It is this high concept that has been reached by

William E. Hulme in his book, *Counseling and Theology,*[36] where he speaks of the right of all persons to the priesthood and of the greatest act by which we perform our Christian service to the other, being a priest in his own right.

Again, some of the rigid forms under which Christians function make it difficult to permit the redemptive act to be performed in terms of the other one. It is expected that anyone we try to help will be raised at least to our own levels of spiritual insight, doctrinal acceptance, and religious observances. We do not normally, however, reckon with the possibility of their going farther, higher, or wider than the expectancy of our particular religious community. It is inevitable that our witness will be carried on within boundaries already presupposed by us, and these will certainly govern the direction we want the other one to go.

The teacher in the church school faces this problem when subconsciously he uses existing dogma and educational methods as dimensions in which the pupil functions. The pupil is ever responding by testing these boundaries. He knows he needs to be a person and he knows further that this must be accomplished on his own terms. Here as in no other place is the problem of Christian communication lifted up so clearly. The teacher is a person in his own right with feelings, needs, and purposes, which, in teaching, he translates into religious dedication. Further, he has the support of the church's dogma. Apart from the fact that he does not understand it all, and likely takes minor exception to some of the things he does understand, he stands within this dogma. He accepts it as his own and incorporates it into his emotional and spiritual strength.

On the other hand, the pupil speaks only for himself. He knows only that he must grow, and he must do it in the presence of his many teachers. Being a child, he has not learned to withhold or divert his growth energy, and he is so forthright about it that he can succeed in driving the teacher behind a barricade made either of authority ("I'm bigger, better, stronger, or smarter than you!") or of doctrine ("God is bigger, better, stronger, or smarter!"). The one inescapable fact is that these two people need to be the things they are and neither of them will grow unless they permit each other the opportunity for self-realization within the event that brings them together.

In the teaching event, the Christian has the tactical advantage. The pupil is the uninitiated, untrained element. His movements are random, undisciplined, and often wild. Against this the teacher can bring to bear tested and persuasive pressure from the church, the Bible, and the dogma. If the pupil-teacher encounter proceeds with little more than the thrust and counterthrust of these forces, we are probably not far from explaining why the adolescent easily leaves the church. It is his final answer in this sort of dialogue. On the other hand, if the event permitted teacher and learner to "endure" the other, the boundaries would become more permeable. They could be explored, accepted, and improved upon, because each person, more especially the teacher, is "mediator."

Such boundary-setting extends into all aspects of the church's life, and it is especially significant when adults confront one another. For if these boundaries are a threat to the endurance of love, then does not love abound if the boundaries are removed? That the church, operated and controlled by the weakness of human life, could function without the establishment of such boundaries, whether overtly or covertly, is also very unlikely. What it means is that the Christian must decide where to be flexible, at which point he will take a stand, where he will be slowest to compromise, how his concern leads him to move between assertiveness and withdrawal. But above all, the Christian has the one desire in every relationship to duplicate as nearly as possible a redemptive setting in which God can turn life into creative use.

On this basis we are able to trace the creation and re-creation of the church. Given its divine nature and knowing that it is the very body of our Redeemer, it nonetheless has to be translated into the ongoing affairs of men. Therefore, every time the Christian involves another in this redemptive and loving encounter, wherever the table is spread, the arena is opened, and the walls of partition are broken down, there God deigns to give the church. There with his disciples God is again bringing pentecostal power to bear upon us. It is then from this unseen "church" that the seen "church" develops. It will produce all that the church is and does, its service, its worship, its organization, its structure, its concern for teaching, its love of the community. It is not an unlikely theological presupposition that if the acts of incarnation are continued within the conditions under which the Christian communicates, it is also true that the church, the body of Christ, is expressed in this identical way and indeed dependent upon the single and immediate interpersonal relationship.

Love as Hope

The final characteristic of love in the communication event is hope. The word suggests a future condition toward which we are aspiring with anticipation, but to look at it in relationship to the event of love makes the term much more personal and immediate. Christians interested in giving people something to look forward to are also helping them achieve gratification and satisfaction with things within. One of the happiest consequences of loving and being loved is that man can look upon his embarrassment in terms of the ultimate. He is man forgiven, man in joy, man anew, and this is his hope. For the Christian, it is hope that makes belief and endurance possible. It lifts the encounter out of possible decline into gloom and failure. For the seeker, it is "the true light that enlightens every man." It is always "coming into the world."

Look again at the relationship between the Christian and the one in whose life he has become involved. Much that has gone before has made him feel dependent, in need of support from this Christian who has come his way. He trusts him implicitly and is tempted to stop at the point of trust. He will be eager to follow the Christian, go with him to his place of worship, engage in his activities, and seek his destinies after him. What is more, the Christian may be tempted to permit him to do it. Nothing gives us greater satisfaction than to find that our pupils turn out to be pretty much like us. This is salvation without hope, if such an eventuality is possible. It is a journey short of destiny when the seeker finds a plateau of gratification in terms of another. A simple transfer is made from life centered in one's self to life centered in one who looks like a better person.

If one stops on this plateau, he finds that what he has truly done is to place himself in the position where he is already on the threshold of losing himself, not to the earth from which he came, but to another whose life is stronger but whose origin is in the same earth. The Christian senses this; understanding that for a while the needed support is only natural, he is willing to give it. But very gently and with a calculated end in mind, the Christian knows that the greatest hope for his friend is not in his being " like " or " as good as " anyone, but rather in being what ultimately God's Spirit leads him to be. He is given hope of becoming a communicator of and witness to his healing in the same way his own rebirth occurred. He has not only a hope for the future but hope as a condition of his existence. Every sinew of his being now responds in a completely different way to everything around him. He is freed to go into the world, to become a witness in his own right, to communicate as a Christian.

Some Obstacles to Love

To be sure, this may be an oversimplified description of the dynamics by which persons are brought into the Kingdom of God. Moreover, it is too easy to overlook the many resistances and obstacles that exist. We would readily agree that our lack of dedication is the most significant impediment to effective witnessing. However, some obstacles are inherent to the process itself.

First, there is the obstacle of the Christian's involvement

with his own world. We are not always trying to escape our responsibility when we claim we are not good enough to talk to others about the claims of Christ upon their lives. We genuinely feel that the very thing we are trying to communicate is, in ourselves, only partially developed, or its full display is being hampered by counterforces that disturb our sincere wish to be loving. Moreover, knowing our weakness at this point makes us vulnerable to attack from others about our right to communicate the gospel. To forestall this subtle attack upon our own integrity, we choose to keep silent.

Our immaturity, of course, weakens our effectiveness as Christian persons, but on the other hand it is only within the "crucible of outreach" that the technique of loving is ever developed. If we do not find in ourselves this loving acceptance of other people, it is probably due to the fact that it has not had sufficient practice within our lives and that we are forfeiting our right to speak for God in spite of our handicaps. For many of us, our tragic silence is due not so much to repeated failure in trying to engage people in a dialogue of faith, but rather to our fear of failure which prevents us from starting the process. Perfection is not a requirement in the gesture toward the other. What is required, however, is that we earnestly seek to govern our lives and to believe in a world that governs its life by these deep-lying acts of godliness. The acceptance of our own weakness is part of the built-in relationship, for within this pattern of endurance the person comes to learn that he has company in his quest for truth, and that his companion is characterized by the same deep-lying motives and aspirations that have been present in his own life.

The second obstacle is found in the fact that we need to perform the art of relationship largely by means of the most obscure type of human expression – speech. There is probably more "tower of Babel" in one language than in all the combination of languages in the world. Not that we do not know the words we are using, but we do not always know what they mean. There is something exceedingly private about the language we grow up to accept and use as our own. We actually talk many languages. Our families have their private words that are meaningless to the outsider. Think of the groups to which we belong and we are thinking of as many " languages." It is through all this confusion that love has to work. From every new " event," though it may be composed of only two persons, there emerges a new language that is difficult to learn because persons are more apt to interpret words on the basis of what they mean to themselves than what meaning is intended by the other one.

Wendell Johnson [37] suggests still another aspect to the word obstacle. He indicates that only about six hundred thousand words in our English language exist to symbolize the billions of individual situations that can arise. Of these, however, only a few thousand make up the daily vocabulary of the person. Subtract from these the words used frequently as pronouns, conjunctions, and so on, and there are only a few hundred words left with which to communicate. What this really means is that even in daily life we have to talk about a great many things for which our words are inadequate.

If the surface encounters of life suffer from scarcity of word power, relationship at deeper levels is handicapped even more by structures and formulations that we encounter. It is this kind of obstacle which sometimes will make the church school teacher and the preacher feel rather helpless and hopeless in their role as communicators. If words cannot demonstrate what is truly meant, how then is it possible to use words for intended meanings?

The problem is intensified by the fact that the church itself is the custodian of a special kind of language. If it cannot accurately be called the language of love, it certainly can be called a language about love. The terms used in the Christian church point in the direction of the loving act of God, and while our " light of sacred story " may be very impressive, it is foreign to the person who has not grown up in the family. However, it would hardly do to give up our terminology, for something as great as love needs many five-syllable words to do it justice. But terminology still remains an obstacle, and we cannot feel that we are successfully communicating as Christians if we permit this obstacle to go unnoticed. One answer is found in the discussion in the last chapter of the full range of man's expression. The teacher does not have to be all talk; nor does the minister; nor does any Christian. We possess a thousand types of self-extension to accompany language that carry with them the same loving gesture as our words: the simple gesture of being in another's presence, of feeling that it is good to be standing with him, of laughing when he laughs, being sorry when he is filled with sorrow; of the soft smile in the presence of harsh words, of the uncritical appraisal of life in general, the acceptance of what is being given to one without rancor or ill will. For the church school teacher it naturally means that there will be an extreme broadening of his entire movement among the people with whom he affiliates and with whom he has the responsibility of teaching. He will not be afraid of the awkwardness of silence in the session where persons are encouraged to think for themselves. Most of our church school sessions and even services of worship proceed on somewhat the same basis as radio programs, whose broadcasters have to be apologetic if they run into twenty seconds of silence.

We have not heretofore spoken about silence as a form of communication, but it is one of the most powerful. A few years ago several seminary students were involved in a group therapy session with a professor. The session was designed to help the students with emotional problems that were hindering their seminary program. After the tenth session the professor called for some comments about the progress of the group and asked for critical evaluation of the various aspects of the group's procedure. One boy whose feelings of inferiority were so deep that he was literally threatened in all his human associations said he liked the silence better than any other aspect of the group activity. When asked why, he replied, "It made me feel equal to everyone else." One can call attention to the matters at hand by silence every bit as effectively as he can by rapping or calling for attention, or otherwise begging for it with noise. Moreover, silence calls out nuances of understanding and appreciation for which no words can be found.

Most of all, however, the barrier of language is overcome by the gesture of service. Our urges to perform "deeds of kindness" for one another have fallen upon hard times. We are somewhat in the position of one who has to buy a Christmas present for someone who "has everything." What does one give another in a society where the needs of all of us are met more than adequately? In fact, it may be an insult to assume that persons need something from our hand, or that we can be of service to anyone except the very poor, or the very downtrodden, or the very ill. But have we forgotten that it is the giver and not the gift that really counts? Is it not true that the alerted and listening person will soon be able to detect in another's life some of the lacks, the sheer material lacks, that one might be able to fulfill? This is a language all its own. Every person has his soft point of interest, the place where the gesture toward him can be made by an overt act of giving. And this is the kind of language fully understood by anyone who lives on this earth. The little child who is surrounded by all kinds of gifts at Christmas time can be weaned away from them by an uncle who, before he gives the gift, has thought what it must be like to be a child, and chooses it accordingly.

The lack of proper speech through which to portray our Christian concerns and the accompanying feeling of inferiority concerning our approach to other people provide the basis for a third reason why our approach to people seems inadequate and ineffective. The metaphor of the Christian religion is extremely difficult. There are some very basic religious assertions that yield to no amount of logical or verifiable description. When we talk to someone about the Christian life, we are working in areas that are boundless, and not measurable by standards we use for other things. In our desire for the certain, the tried, and the true, we too frequently require our religious beliefs to fit similar patterns. Moreover, some religious interpretation offers unqualified answers to the most persistent uncertainties mankind faces. Moreover, these are agreed upon by the Christian community and the continuous emphasis upon them makes us feel guilty if we attempt to engage in a relationship where they are disregarded. It is a prevailing world view that everything is somehow accounted for within natural law and can be subjected to measurement and experimental techniques. This view is invested with considerable emotion, and the communicator is pulled in two directions — toward retrenchment in the familiar paths established by the "proved" truth, and toward the free and open encounter where there is much ambiguity.

K. G. Collier, in an article, "Obstacles to Religious Belief," in the *Hibbert Journal*, describes in the extreme the image of the church. Professor Collier says:

> In my view of the current picture (which does not represent my own feelings), the myth of the church is of an institution which is like a dowager out of touch with modern realities, clinging to semblance of the past authority; which holds a faith similar to the children's belief in Father Christmas and teaches a naïve morality suitable for Sunday schools, and which generally expects adults to be willing to go on taking a somewhat junior status in the organization. The clergy are thought of as merely being lucky to have an easy job.[38]

Professor Collier goes on to suggest these solutions. First, that the authority of the church be revised downward so that the whole church feels a sense of obligation for witnessing to the gospel. Second, the more informal approach to evangelism wherein we stand with the inquirer and chat about nothing, whether at work or at leisure, and yet enable him to raise the great questions of human life and destiny. Third, the need to study the actual virtues in modern life and learn how to build upon them in talking with nonbelievers.

Christians have difficulty revising at all what the church

feels it has an obligation to defend and declare, let alone revising it "downward." It holds us together and our certainty that it will hold others together transcends the concern for a methodology such as Professor Collier suggests in his second point, to be casual and leisurely about our relationship to other people. This is not the way of the church. Although it may fail to attain the goal, we want to imagine the church as upright and direct, with a swift and certain message that goes straight to the heart of the matter; nothing casual about the church, nothing indefinite, nothing unsure, unplanned, or unaccounted for. For the Sunday school teacher to involve himself in thinking all week about the great questions of life, and then to walk into his class on Sunday morning and say, "I have just been thinking about a couple of things I wanted to talk to you about and get your opinion on this morning," is hardly to be thought of. If it is thought of, it dies for the lack of a good conscience in doing it, for we are bound by "tried and true" techniques that view casualness as noncurricular. As necessary as it is to maintain an absolute point of reference for life, is it possible that in his witness, the Christian can be casual, or even unsure?

It is a long, hard pilgrimage into the heart of the community of God's people. The closer the outsider gets to it the more he is aware of the language, customs, and loyalties. In his conversation with the Christian, he had the feeling of gradual liberation from the strictures of his inner slavery, and maybe also from his preconceptions concerning the rigidity of the church and the people in it. Now he is overtaken by the tradition of well-formulated practice and thought. He has now a new reason to feel uncomfortable and defensive. His hope lies in two directions: one, that his newly found resources will help him tolerate the immaturity of others, even in the church; and two, that communication among Christians will become more cordial and inviting to the world, and that more and more we shall embody the doctrine that sustains us. Or, as Paul Johnson puts it:

To bear the name of " Christian " is not so genuine a sign as to express the Christian spirit in attitudes and acts of unselfish love. Deeper than the verbal level of identity and communication is the dynamic motive power of identification and community. A person who expresses a Christian spirit of love is a contagious center of enlarging community fellowship.[39]

Chapter V

Christian Talks to Christian

To isolate the instances in which Christian talks to Christian is nearly impossible, for in our "Christian nation" there are few human encounters where Christians are not talking to one another, even though they are unaware of it. However, our vocational and social contacts involve us in a great many contacts that do not require penetration to the level of the meaning of the Christian faith we talked about in the last chapter. In reality such experiences will of necessity be few for all of us. On the other hand, the Christian needs to communicate at these levels as a matter of his own devotion and growth. He needs the give-and-take with others whose meanings and language give satisfying reassurance to his faith. This chapter intends, therefore, to look at the way conversation takes place between Christian and Christian within their religious community, and how this differs from the conversation the Christian carries on in other relationships.

The Magic of Sunday Morning

Communication between Christians occurs frequently. We meet together to administer the work of the church, for fellowship, service, and other "meetings," which are part and parcel of the church's ongoing task. However, once each week Christians meet with fellow Christians as a matter of course. Apart from all other gatherings on the church's calendar, there is some "magic" about Sunday morning. It is then that the community comes together. Words are spoken that are understood by all; or, if not understood, they are at least comforting. It is here that the majority of the citizenry turns its thoughts when the church is mentioned or when its life is in any way alluded to. It is out of this Sunday morning event that all other aspects of the church's life are created. Every Christian shares in some way in these events, either as a leader, an active participant, or an earnest spectator. A set of agenda is built out of our work together and Christians help create it. After years of their functioning together, a structure takes form and an at-homeness is created, which seem different from any other structure and any other at-homeness within the secular community.

And who can deny that there is much talk, both planned and unplanned? Words of greeting, instruction, bidding, announcement, are joined with song, prayer, praise, admonition, confession, and dedication. At times one person speaks and others listen, and the casual observer might get the impression that at other times everyone is talking and no one is listening. In small churches, classes of instruction are separated by curtains of talk. The words are accompanied by movement, gesture, and signs. There is little complete silence and even less complete stillness.

" Christian with Christian" and "Christian with the World"

When comparing " Christian with Christian," and " Christian with the world," one of the most apparent differences is derived from a development in our culture, that still carries for the Christian some very significant meaning. It is found in the mood of the Sunday morning and of the church as a whole. In spite of the fact that commercialization has gradually made inroads upon the Sunday morning, for the Christian there is something happening that does not take place other mornings. This mood may begin with one of the most unheralded of all our behavior patterns that is prelude to religious observance. There is not a simple coincidence between the fact that at least twenty-four hours prior to our going to church most of us feel it necessary to bathe ourselves, and when we arise on Sunday morning we are apt to put on not only clean clothes, but good clothes, and we somehow assume that the others we greet will have done the same. It would be a rare thing indeed for people to appear in church the way they appear at their work or at other engagements of their life. Children, especially, may even be required to undergo some degree of discomfort to appear in their "Sunday best." Even when ministers attempt to get people together on an informal basis in their so-called working clothes, or try to build services on a "come as you are" basis, the results are usually quite "underwhelming." People feel that a *mood* for worship, a *mood* of church going, is essential. This mood is carried over into the church itself. Its sights, its smells, its noise, are ingredients in the entire mood structure. It is a reverential mood, or at least designed to move people in the direction of a reverence for what is to occur and the things handled in the acts of devotion.

Little argument is necessary to show how important the understanding of this mood really is to the person who wishes to communicate within it. Our very speech will be governed by it. The loudness of our voice, the inflections, intonations, and the types of signals we send will be governed by the mood that has been created not only for this Sunday in particular, but for all Sundays in all years past of which we are now an active inheritor. This mood is significant if we are to understand how the Christian must act, speak, and extend himself in the church when he talks to his fellow Christians.

The second difference lies in the presuppositions people have about themselves and others around them when they meet together in the church. As Seward Hiltner [40] has pointed out, there would be no reality to salvation, redemption, and the new being in Jesus Christ if this did not make a difference in the things that happen when Christians get together. It is on this very point that most of our argument must rest for the proposition we shall make a little later on, that what takes place inside the church among Christians, when and if they are truly Christian, may even affect some of the basic processes of communication. Of course, the prime difficulty in establishing this position is encountered in the fact that when Christian meets Christian on Sunday morning or at any time in his church experience, we should suppose he is truly Christian. But this is a precarious supposition, for in the church Christians are apt to be pretty much the same as they are anywhere. Were we to roam around within the church structure at any given time when Christians are meeting with their fellow Christians, we would notice that some little groups seem friendly and warm. Others show signs of tension. Among some people there is a close relationship, and conversation passes easily between them. Among others the relationships seem more distant. They say little to each other. They hear little. They sit in their own little islands of separate concern. The Christian might suddenly become aware that even in the community of God's people there are deep interpersonal struggles.

In *Life Together*, Dietrich Bonhoeffer describes what we all have seen and even been party to in the church.

> It is vitally necessary that every Christian community from the very outset face this dangerous enemy squarely, and eradicate it. There is no time to lose here, for from the first moment when a man meets another person, he is looking for a strategic position he can assume and hold over against that person. There are strong persons and weak ones. If a man is strong, he immediately claims the right of the weak as his own and uses it against the strong. There are gifted and ungifted persons, simple people and difficult people, devout and less devout, the sociable and the solitary. Does not the ungifted person have to take up a position just as well as the gifted person, the difficult one as well as the simple? And if I am not gifted, then perhaps I am devout anyhow; or if I am not devout, it is only because I do not want to be. May not the sociable individual carry the field before him and put the timid, solitary man to shame? Then may not the solitary per-

son become the undying enemy and ultimate vanquisher of the sociable adversary? Where is there a person who does not with instinctive sureness find the spot where he can stand and defend himself, but which he will never give up to another, for which he will fight with all the drive of his instinct of self-assertion?

All this can occur in the most polite or even pious environment.[41]

While none of us is completely immune from these involvements simply because we are all human, yet it is within this fellowship that we presume to act differently, or at least assume that human encounter should be different.

We are sensitive to the need to function on a different level. We are doing things in one another's presence which are not duplicated anywhere else in the society. The church, the fellowship of the new being, is in session, and when Christian talks to Christian there is an invitation to another Presence, a kind of vertical reach that characterizes them in ways different from those outside the church. This takes us back to our earlier assumptions about the nature of communication itself. At its deepest levels it taps the basic meanings of all of life. Where did I come from? Where am I going? Who is God? What does he mean to me? Where does he intend me to go? These are not simply academic questions. They are matters of meaning. They are matters of mood. Even though we reduce the number of Christians who can actually talk to one another on this level to the bare minimum, it remains true that within the fellowship of Christian people this is the understructure upon which all our words are framed and our personalities are related.

To be sure, we must frown upon easy assumptions about one another. The simple statements, "I am a Christian," or "He is a Christian," do not get us very far if we are attempting to implement the deepest type of communication. What this does mean, however, is that when Christians meet for any purpose whatsoever and recognize among themselves the knowledge of the presence of a new being in Christ, the presence of Christ's own Spirit, there is a quality of relationship hardly possible among others. Here is discovered one of the most subtle aspects of Christian communication, *its ability to be party to the creation and re-creation of the community of God's people.* The church has been created with the sacrifice of our Lord, and has been re-created many times over, but this in no way guarantees its maintenance amongst us. The church is always in the process of being born and reborn within the arena formed by talk, gesture and attentiveness among Christians.

The events of Pentecost are not wholly clear to us, but what is clear is that in the upper room people felt among them the immediacy of Christ's love and sacrifice. They had probably come together as a sort of mourning group, bent on giving condolence to one another at the loss they had suffered. They may even have had in their minds some form of future policy that might be followed. In any event, all their thoughts must have been quite tenuous, grief-ridden, uncertain, and lacking direction. They may have talked at random to one another, and inevitably the conversation must have come around to the realization that whatever they planned would be carried through without the presence of their leader and Lord. From the group then there came a voice that could have said, "You know it seems to me that it is as though he were not dead, that he is right here among us." Another might have taken up the cue and said, "I have been thinking the same thing." And one by one there would have been a testimony to the fact that they had been impressed with the presence of the One who had gone from them, and in that moment of oneness, of the acceptance of this presence, the church was born. This is not only an event upon which all subsequent events were to be predicated. This event is paradigmatic. It is the format of what can occur again and again. When people come together and recognize that they stand in the presence of Christ's Spirit, the church moves into new growth. And so, in a sense, each Sunday morning the church is reborn. It is reborn when, together before God, Christians recognize their mutual need of him; the service they perform is but the collective recognition of their being under God and an attempt to express this relationship through forms of worship. It takes its uniqueness, therefore, from a vertical dimension which it depends upon to structure the intra-Christian community.

The nature of the arena in which Christian talks to Christian constitutes a third difference between this type of communication and communication outside the church. To begin with, like all other social structures, the church develops marks of its uniqueness. Everything within it is designed to make the type of communication it deems advisable easily accomplished. Millions of dollars have been spent to make people feel at home, comfortable, and accepted. Moreover, we have invested great effort to maintain this identity apart from the rest of the world. It is not without significance that the majority of our churches are little islands around which the world flows. They contain windows through which people cannot see (either way) and are guarded by the kind of façade that, while very beautiful and attractive, is not always inviting to the world.

For the stranger, the symbols, forms, and movement are learned only with considerable training. However, for the initiated it is not a difficult experience. It is a warm and inviting place. While it is true that there are many people on the rolls of the church who move easily between the church and the world in their allegiances, it is also true that within the church there are countless thousands for whom the most tragic things would have to occur before they could be persuaded to leave it. They are acquainted with the structure. They have not only an emotional but a spiritual investment in it. It is the one place where all that religion means to them can be honestly and freely portrayed, with the hope that it will have meaning for their entire lives. They do not panic at words which they cannot understand, for they have heard them so often and realize how harmless and even reassuring they are, that they let them pass as acceptable without full knowledge of their meaning. Neither are they acquainted with all the ramifications of the creeds. Even though they hear from Sunday to Sunday an interpretation of these creeds and beliefs, if they cannot understand them they do not always feel frustrated, because this is home and the intentions of home are always the best.

Here may be one of the reasons why it has traditionally been difficult for the Christian to take his message to the world. Within this structure and arena which he knows so well, he may feel an emotional involvement giving him comfort, providing him an at-homeness to which he has tied a spiritual meaning. He can easily suppose that what he has found in the church is found by other people in other group relationships. He sees the church as a live option among many alternatives in his community, and it just " happens " that tradition has set him into the church rather than into some other form of community structure where likely the same thing happens to others. Out of this has come a type of " live and let live " attitude among Christians who are not too eager to press the point of the church upon people. If other forms of social arrangement are providing for them what the church provides for the Christian, then it may not be too important even to invite allegiance to the spiritual community. On the other hand, however, if the Christan sees that in this community a unique function is being played and unique processes are at work in which the guidance of God's Spirit is sought for undergirding, the church then becomes a structure with some unique significance. The tendency of our churches to look like other group formations in the culture does not help us develop an understanding of the basic structure of the people of God. Therefore, Christians in them are apt not to take themselves any more seriously than if they were applying similar energies to other forms of social good will and service.

Does it make any difference when a community becomes a loving community? Is there a basic change that takes place in an organizational structure when it is dominated by the force of love? It is difficult to answer these questions, but they do make us wonder whether the very nature of the spirit that holds Christians together does not have something to say about the language, structure, thought forms, and functioning of their community. We rob the people of God of uniqueness if we define the administrative, worship, and educational work of the church in terms alien to the constant structuring and restructuring of human events based on love. The Christian will govern all his behavior in these terms. He will relate to groups, terms, ideas, hymns, the central Word, in ways different from all other of his experiences, no matter where he goes. The difference develops habit patterns of knowing how to behave, when to speak, and when not to speak. If, in other situations, he is prone to lose control of his basic emotions, within the structure of the church he may make an effort to maintain these controls. He will even help in some way to construct the arena where the dynamics of love will be deepened.

With the increasing emphasis upon lay participation, it is the rare person who does not feel obliged to become involved in the life of the church. It is the genius of Protestantism that the responsibility for the structure and function of the church falls upon every person.

Failure to bring the " loving gesture " into all aspects of the church's life will have at least two consequences. First, in order to ensure his feeling of at-homeness, the Christian becomes more deeply rooted in the speech, forms, and customs of the community, and after years of association he accepts the arena of the church as something " special " in his life. When he enters its doors he becomes a special kind of communicator. His speech is returned in kind. He has different expectancies. He primes himself to make the proper responses and expects to elicit from others responses he understands. This exchange of symbols becomes closely identified with the structure in which he worships and he comes to feel that it is in the structure *and only in the structure* that he can use these terms and be understood. The church then becomes a cloistered and "secret" organization, not because it is in fact, but simply because within the church itself the structure of communication has symbolic meaning which cannot easily be transferred to any other group in the society.

The second consequence will be felt by the one seeking admission to the fellowship. Perhaps one of the most crucial steps in the evangelistic enterprise is taken at the point of transition from the nonchurch community into the community of Christians. In the one-to-one relationship, the seeker has become familiar with the Christian "person" whose ways he has mastered. He assumes that all Christians and groups of Christians will be the same, or nearly so. Being nurtured in his first steps through love, concern, and rudimentary Christian thought, he is not wholly prepared to confront the full range of the church's activity. If, therefore, this new relationship is too difficult for him to negotiate, and he cannot quickly and easily enough adapt to the pattern, he will be repelled. On the other hand, in the church whose people have "revised downward" their common spirit to meet the initiate with the same freedom he felt with the single Christian, the transition will be made with little difficulty. Even within its own border, the church will need to maintain above all its interest in its uniqueness – the ability to act out of love.

The third difference is a conclusion reached from these two, and can best be stated in the form of a question. Is this difference in communication within and without the church simply one of form and degree, or does it constitute a qualitative matter that affects even the deepest aspects of communication and calls forth certain processes that may not be at work in any other place. Seward Hiltner [42] has contended that the basic processes of communication are unchanged, no matter where we find them. Basically, this would have to be agreed with. It is true that speech is speech, no matter where it is used. We hear things, we send signals and receive responses, and perform the acts of simple communication very much the same no matter where we are. The body and all of its equipment will be with us as long as we live, and where and however we live, irrespective of the nature of our lives.

Something more should be said, however, about the process of communication. If by process we simply mean the techniques by which our ideas are thrown toward one another, then we would probably have to admit that there is no difference between communication process among Christians and between Christians and the world. However, process must take on a different meaning when we view it as a means by which we proceed in relationship. At its most basic level, process is dynamic. It is the movement of one element in its natural development being modified through its associations with other elements. It is precisely at this point that the Christian must raise the question as to whether being a Christian means anything about the processes by which he communicates. If process is dynamic, are the fundamental dynamics at work among Christians different from the dynamics at work when a Christian is in relationship with one not Christian?

To press the question farther, when a Christian and a non-Christian are in conversation and suddenly recognize themselves to be one with God in a common quest of the knowledge of his love and will, does something happen to the processes of communication so that what went on before in the give-and-take of verbal and auditory signal-giving and reponse now has taken on a new and more fundamental element? Does something unique occur when the Spirit of God, the Judge, the Guide, the Leader, the Convicter, the One who is able in all situations where people meet in his Name, causes the encounter to be on the basis of love? Of course, God's Spirit is present in all forms of communication, but when persons accept that presence and relate in terms of it, a new dimension has been added to anything they do together.

If this be the case within the community of those whose hearts are tuned to the love of God, the processes of communication may be looked at as something other and different from any other form of relationship in the world. This should not be surprising to anyone who fully understands the dynamics of close association. What holds people close to one another? It can be a fear that separation will drive them into aloneness; to prevent this is to hold on with all our might to the thing at hand. People are also held together by a distrust of one another, by a lack of sincere surrender to each other, or a lack of feeling of at-homeness within the presence of the other. Or, because of fear people may simply be dependent upon one another, knowing that any significance in their own lives is derived from the significance put there by another. To this can be added other forces that bring people together, and each brings with it its own dynamic. Things are expressed in guarded tones; meanings that do not exist will be read into every word. The process of give-and-take operates on a dynamic of distrust, hatred, and fear. Resentments will well up but if the need for one another is great enough they will be repressed. Still they cannot remain hidden because the process of communication itself is the most subtle revealer of all that takes place " underneath " in our lives.

Suppose, however, that people are drawn together on the basis of love. Rather than being guarded, our language is free. We do not need to press for our integrity, for we know it is accepted by the other simply because he is Christian. We do not need to protect ourselves from the threats of another because we know that the other is looking upon us in terms of love. In this kind of relationship, it seems almost certain that the consequences will be in an entirely different form of communication. The resistance, the guarded language, the failure to interpret correctly, all give way to the fruits of the spirit, which are joy, patience, long-suffering, kindness, meekness. These in themselves are processes. It may even make a difference in the way we speak. It certainly makes a difference in the things we hear. It makes a difference in the way our eyes fall upon another. It makes a difference in our greeting. It affects the total make-up of the body, and even though we do not need new equipment to accomplish the change, the processes by which the equipment is set into motion and the dynamics at work in them certainly will be changed.

The Loving Community in Action

It is common knowledge that the church bears its share of criticism for not being truly Christian. This, of course, makes whatever logic is in the foregoing suffer some practical setbacks. It would be assumed that it takes a perfect Christian to communicate in the way just described. "Perfect love casts out fear," resentment, hostility, and distrust, but who among us is willing to stand up and declare that in his own life these have been cast out? Are we not then thrown back upon the argument that, after all, the church is just another organization, that we are deluding ourselves in talking about a loving community when the persons in it are so far removed from the qualities which go to make up love? Two things need to be said here.

First, it is quite probable that this spirit of love occurs more frequently than we suspect. Two men meet on the ramp at an airport. They are planning to take the same plane to another city. They have never seen each other before, and unknown to each other is the fact that each has deep orientation in the Christian community. Each is active in the work of his church and each is attempting to build his life within the love of God and his revelation in Christ. For a while they chat casually and agree to be seated together on the plane if this is possible. Soon they are settled and conversing. It is not long before each reveals the fact that he is interested in the church. This sets them off in a deeper discussion of their problems of being Christian and at the same time negotiating with an unchristian society. For an hour and a half this conversation proceeds. When it begins to veer away from matters having to do with the Christian life, it soon comes back, and for the duration of the flight two Christians find themselves in an experience of sharing. Differences of opinion were met with interest and understanding. Each was trying to learn from the other. The flight ends. They may never see each other again, but for an hour and a half there was a strange and enlightening give-and-take between two Christians.

There are some interesting things to notice about this encounter. First of all, it was not long after they met until each began to move with instinctive accuracy toward the other in terms of a religious motivation. They would not have been satisfied to maintain their conversation at a more casual level. The other thing to observe is that the entire conversation was maintained with the processes of communication functioning within a free relationship. To be sure, neither of these men got to know the other as well as he might. They had not worked on committees together in church. They did not have the opportunity to observe one another at close range and perhaps become annoyed with some of the attitudes or behavior of each other. But this is precisely the point. When these two men parted they had reinforced within themselves the fact it is possible to engage in give-and-take on the level of a Christian spirit. Neither of them felt he had to defend himself. Neither of them was constantly aware of his inferiority or his inadequacy before the other. Their Christian concerns gave them a common ground bounded on all sides by a concept of love within which they were attempting to relate to each other. This sort of event is not unusual. It occurs more frequently than we think. Such casual meeting of Christian with Christian, especially where the involvements are not too deep, encourages us to go deeper in our own experiences with others and gives us the assurance that the processes of love are much more significant and productive than the processes that grow out of our feelings of fear and resentment.

The second way this spirit of love is at work is to be found within the church itself. It is difficult for a group of people to have prolonged association without developing a love for one another, especially if they are constantly confronted with its necessity. This love may work in strange ways, and on the surface may appear to be anything but love. Where else but in the Christian community can people whose imperfect attitudes and immature behavior are known to one another still work together and press toward understanding and mutual accord? Meeting these problems of attitude failure is, of course, very difficult. However, the Christian meets them, puts up with them, and sustains a relationship in spite of them, demonstrating thereby what is probably most characteristic of the love of God in human life. To be sure, some people are hurt to the point where they can no longer tolerate the fellowship, but Christians as Christians do not find that these disturbances are the end of all things. The resources of love are brought to bear and it is the life of the church itself, a prolonged association with people whom we come to know and understand, that makes it possible to move toward creative and productive tasks, in spite of the fact that we do not always express a kind of behavior that seems to be founded in love.

Movement toward a Christian community will be closely related to the image the Christian has of himself in the church. To assume that it should be easy to act like a Christian in the life of the church is to reckon without knowledge of what happens in long-established groups. It is only in the most casual and fortuitous human association that people are not classified according to office and function, and the church is neither casual nor fortuitous. From its beginning it has appointed "some to be prophets, some to be teachers," on down (chronologically) to trustees, deacons, and a host of other functionaries. Each of these designations creates a "second image" through which the Christian will filter his words and gestures.

For example, the term "teacher" suggests the traditional picture of an "up front" person, verbal and intelligent, who can prepare a lesson for other people, and take them through a series of studies on almost anything pertaining to the life and faith of the church. With such an impressive job analysis, it is little wonder that this "second image" will get in the way of the "first image"—that of being Christian. The teacher then must handle two images of himself, and often he requires the second to give meaning to the first. His place in the Christian community is authenticated by his performance of delegated tasks. This is expected and even natural. Without specific positions and structure in the church, its tasks would not be performed nor would its life be built and maintained.

It is only when the Christian's image of himself *as a Christian* is lost in a role to be played in the fellowship that danger arises and Christian communication is threatened. Seward Hiltner [43] has suggested three areas in which the church is always at work: (1) learning, understanding, or instructing, (2) realizing, deepening, or edifying, and (3) celebrating, reminding, or commemorating. This listing is useful in that it keeps the *task* of the Christian close to the *meaning* of the Christian. When Christians speak to one another, the fact that we are teachers is secondary to the more basic fact that, as Christians, we are responsible for mutual instruction and enlightenment. Being a leader has meaning only because all Christians must deepen and edify the lives of other Christians. Even the minister, who bears the chief responsibility for the conducting of worship, knows he does this, not because he is the designated leader, but because as a Christian he must join in the celebration and holy offerings of the body of Christ.

The " Second Image "

The official designations within the church will persist. Without them we should lose valuable " points of reference " for the task of intercommunication. They are symbols of the movement of the acts of mutual love and concern expected of all Christians. Being symbols, however, they are " second images " and should not lose touch with the realities they represent. A look at some of the offices of the Christian might help bring symbol and reality together.

The teacher. The teacher has fallen upon hard times in our society. Elsewhere [44] I have indicated some of the problems that have arisen in our churches in terms of the teacher. Because of the fact that we have grown to appreciate the democratic processes within the life of the church there has been a tendency to frown upon "authoritarian" techniques and with some degree of justification, for the teacher is the symbol of authority. On the other hand, however, minimizing the teacher has done something to the nature of "learning, understanding, and instructing" among Christians. Without question, the teacher is a necessary intrusion in the life of every generation. Whether done formally or informally makes little difference. To disregard the responsibility that a teacher has in the work of the church or the performance of any group functioning in our society is to invite catastrophe and the sudden discontinuation of the processes of living itself.

In the church the teacher functions at two levels. First, on the level of communicating through instruction. Here the teacher stands at an exceedingly strategic position in the ongoing work of the church as a mature element in possession of the knowledge of its traditions, thought patterns, forms, the reason why it does the things it does and stands for the things it stands. He has surrounding him the fellowship of these people, who have learned from previous generations the importance of this group, who have assimilated its history, who are familiar with its life. The teacher stands as the "intruder" between what the church knows about itself and does not know about itself. The number of techniques of teaching are legion and it is not to the credit of the church that most of them have been taken over from other areas of society and not formulated within the Christian community.[45] It is in this sort of situation that the teacher feels he has a certain responsibility for the "communication of," to use Hendrik Kraemer's[46] term. He has a message. It is given to him through his curriculum. He is responsible for absorbing it and then somehow translating it for the group of students on Sunday morning. In this type of communication the teacher has the responsibility for the performance of a specific task that is heavily charged with content and theological form, so that it is almost necessary for him to use techniques that will get across to the person as quickly and efficiently as possible the information the church has about itself.

The teacher engaged in such an enterprise will have an image of himself as a go-between. He is in a mediating position between the church and the person. He speaks not his own voice but the voice of the tradition. If he could remove all emotional content, all his basic presuppositions about the nature of communication, he would see himself, more than in any other responsibility he bears in the church, standing at a place where, on the one hand, he echoes what has gone before in the church and what it is attempting to do, and, on the other hand, the person who must learn these things. To achieve these ends, the methodology of the church's educational enterprise will not differ greatly from any group in the society whose task is to pass on to every new generation information about itself. Therefore the teacher is under obligation to teach the logic and content of the faith as readily and conveniently as possible. He knows how people learn, he knows what techniques are best understood by persons and how they can best develop their capacities to absorb information; and he applies these techniques to his teaching. It is not difficult to instruct. Indeed it has been reduced to a science of communicating through audio and visual signals, through adequate preparation and presentation of the curriculum at the correct level of the student's understanding, which almost assure that the person will learn the things the church deems it important for him to know.

Moreover, the teacher has incorporated this content into his own life. Since the teacher's position and image have been weakened because of an identification with authority, he is reluctant to assert and affirm his own life. He feels that authenticating himself in the presence of others will achieve little; hence, he cannot be himself, a condition indispensable to good communication. Although there has been no planned effort to bring it about, Christians generally and teachers in particular have abandoned the policy of telling " what God has done for me." One knows all the risks involved in turning loose upon the immature a barrage of personal testimony which can easily degenerate into ego-gratifying self-praise; yet the teacher still stands before a group with his own life. This does not mean, of course, that the teacher becomes a constant articulator of his status before God, for the articulation of it probably defeats its very meaning. Nor does it mean that the teacher will take time explaining how things are with him beyond the necessity of establishing a free relationship with the pupil. But it does mean that there is in the teacher no fear of being a person in his own right. His feelings, the ideas that come to him, and the overtones of his own mood, are all available for use in the learning situation. Love permits us to express ourselves. The child learns much when he sees a loving person act out his life within the control of love.

The leader. In the church, the leader has this designation because either through appointment or election he has been commissioned to assume a responsibility for performing some specific task. The tasks vary, but in all cases, on the basis of strictly formal relationships, the duties are well defined and the procedures by which the tasks are performed are not particularly difficult. The church is " big business " and one can hear repeatedly that the work of the church should be carried on in a businesslike way, which means again that the church is not a unique community in the sheer task of planning, executing, and evaluating its program. The " second image " of the church leader is not hard to come by. It is an easy carry-over from his familiar patterns of behavior in the world.

The worker. This term has a very general meaning for persons in the church and embraces almost anything anyone does, including just attending the gatherings of the fellowship with regularity. But it generally refers to a person who is faithful and helpful within a specific parish. The term may include teachers or leaders, but also it may include persons who somehow or other add weight or influence to the more obscure or unheralded aspects of the church's life. The persons who sing in the choir, visit in the parish, usher, bake pies, give the church a periodic house cleaning, or in one way or another let their hand be given to the work of the church, might generally be defined as "church workers." This includes about everyone. It is only the deliberately recalcitrant person who does not permit himself in one way or another to be drawn into the work of the church. In order to escape involvement, he would have to stay away altogether, and even then he would find himself solicited for some other form of tenuous attachment to the program.

What this amounts to is that all these people have been given a formal relationship to the church, and it is precisely at this point where the church asserts its greatest influence in maintaining itself. The church has become "task"-oriented. It has "work" to do and its people have the image of themselves as "church workers," and from this self-image communication among Christians is carried on. We even discuss improving communication on this basis. We discuss how to have better meetings and how to have more open and permissive group situations in which people learn. As rapidly as possible we improve the mass media of religion in order to make the things of the church available to a wider audience. Church architecture is developed with an eye to assisting in the performance of our task as teachers, as leaders, as workers. Each teacher has his curriculum, each leader his manual, each worker his particular way of doing the thing that he is supposed to do, each choir member his folio, each worship director his liturgy, and equipped with these paraphernalia we understand ourselves to be good church workers. We have a great deal of assistance available to help us to communicate on these bases and on these terms. We get help not only from within the church but probably more so from areas outside, where work is also carried on by an organizational structure that a group of people must maintain in order to produce and create.

The "First Image"

Now let us look at these three groups of people on the basis of the "first image." What we do as teachers, workers, and leaders will be uniquely Christian only if, in carrying out these offices, communication takes place out of concern and love. Whatever is unique in the "second image" will be derived from the uniqueness of the "first image." Moreover, simply to understand the difference between these levels and even to make a serious attempt to bring our "task images" under control of Christian impulses will serve only to deal with the problem at the surface level. More deeply involved is the fact that much of the total impact we make in the Christian community is unplanned. At any given time, each Christian is enlightening, teaching, edifying, celebrating, or otherwise witnessing out of his "first image." We have no choice. When we are asked to teach in the school of the church, this is not a new venture. It is simply being asked to do in a planned and formal way what we have been doing all along. In the same way we lead, work, stimulate, and effect the feeling tone of the Christian community. It could be that when we are asked to teach or otherwise lead in the church too much is made of the uniqueness of the position. If we could see a continuation of basic Christian function in such a transition, we might forestall the devastating effects of the teacher's losing the "first image" of himself as a Christian.

How do the teacher, leader, and worker carry on their tasks of communicating at the level of Christian love? How can the Christian maintain contact between the two self-images under which he needs to function? The answer comes when the Christian sees his task only as the fulfillment of the Christian meanings given to all tasks. Let us look again at the three tasks from this perspective.

The first is *nurturing*. This goes on whether it is planned or not. In some way the very young learn very early how close they can get to us before we become impatient with them.

Either they draw from us a living faith that sustains them within the church, or they find little or nothing in us and simply bide their time until they are permitted to select other groups that accept them. A relationship of the mature to the immature is found within the church to a degree that it is not found outside the church. When Christian speaks to non-Christian outside the church, the encounter is usually between peers. Within the church, however, there is opportunity for an unusual relationship between the adult and the child. In fact, probably more than in any other group in the society the church is composed of nearly an identical number of each. In itself, this constant interparticipation and interaction of mature with immature is sufficient to make communication of Christian with Christian exceedingly important. When there are added to this the encounter between mature Christians and the relationship between the experienced Christian and the novices in the community, the amount of learning that takes place is quite impressive.

What is the nurturing process? How do Christians nurture one another? Those who are new to the church at first have feelings of "lostness," discomfort, ignorance, and constant embarrassment. The smallest child, although familiar with the buildings and the essential processes of our religious community, is not yet familiar with its thought patterns. For a long time both child and novice know only what they feel. They understand only what they sense to be the mood of those around them and probably more than in any other way they are nurtured in the faith by being in the presence of the mature.

What happens then when a mature Christian and an immature Christian confront each other? Here we go back to what was said about the fundamentals of the communication system. These must work here and work at their very best. We must be attentive. When we speak, our words and ideas give integrity both to ourselves as Christians and to the faith we represent. Moreover, the mature person recognizes that the encounter of the mature with the immature brings nurture and understanding to both. This can be accomplished only when each person is permitted to be himself in the presence of the other.

The teacher, for instance, carries a tremendous weight of information. He may even be threatening to the little child because of the superiority of his knowledge and experience (not to speak of his size and manner). It is easy for a teacher to develop an "over"- relationship, not only because he is more experienced than the immature but also because he is in the superior position of having prepared and of controlling the things to be taught. This is true also within the fellowship of adults, where the teacher has the advantage of being the learned one, the one who is looked to for leadership, the establisher of the level of communication in which the nurturing process takes place. Therefore it seems only reasonable that the whole area of our teaching within the church must come under frequent and serious evaluation. We need to know whether or not along with our instructive processes we are also in the process of nurturing, and whether our communication permits the immature to be themselves, unhindered by such a weight of terminology and symbolism that good communication is frustrated.

The neophyte does not yet know the words. Simply coming into the church and accepting the Christian way is not a guarantee that he has understood the language of the church. He will not respond immediately to the words that for us have been familiar. He will want to raise questions about them, but he hesitates to be cast in a bad light. He may even assume that words and ideas about Christian love will be as easily understood as is the feeling of love. In any event, it will be hard for him to accept the fact that the words about Christian love are more exciting and meaningful than the events in which love is demonstrated. In reviewing its language, the church will want to know what words and ideas can easily be related to the new Christian's first image of himself. Christian nurture presupposes a family spirit; the development of a mood in which the freedom of the person is guaranteed; and movement among Christians assuring him of training from those who share his needs, so that he can engage in the process of growth without threat or embarrassment. This is true permissiveness. When persons are dominated by love, permissiveness is dominated by it. Permissiveness is not license or impulse, but rather a creative movement toward the fulfillment of personality and the accomplishment of the will of God within the arena of love.

Among Christians growth in learning and understanding is not confined to the young and the new. It is an endless process, witnessed to by the fact that the church, unlike other cultural groups, provides formal training for its entire constituency. This does not mean, however, that equal importance is always given to the education of all ages. Rightly, perhaps, we assume that our first energies should be invested in the training of the immature, who need the teacher as a requirement for the initial structuring of their belief systems. Moreover, it is assumed that enlightenment and growth among mature Christians develop through more casual peer relationships. It is on this very assumption that the hope for learning and instruction will finally have to rest. The excellent results coming out of adult education should make the church sensitive to the ways adults can "grow in the grace and knowledge of our Lord." Without minimizing the formal aspects of this process, we should press for a clearer understanding of how we "teach" one another in those events where communication between Christians is normal and free.

In the first place, whatever else they accomplish, the formal aspects of learning will need to become occasions for Christians to witness to one another. Christian growth takes place only by difficult and tedious steps out of firmly held and emotionally supported patterns of thought and behavior. It is probably more difficult for the so-called mature to become more mature than for the immature to become mature. In fact, maturity might be defined in terms of the readiness the person possesses, at any age, to grow and learn. Widespread resistance to growth among adults helps formal learning situations generally to become sessions where one can expect existing belief patterns to be reinforced. New words are learned, but the meanings change little. In part, this type of educational method must bear responsibility for the development of the "closed" language that moves farther and farther away from the world.

Our difficulty is not so much with "formal" education as it is with "formal" people. It is generally the teacher with a vivid "second image" who leads the formal sessions in the church away from the exploration of meaning. In small groups, Christians can be helpful to one another in reinterpreting and redefining the gospel in terms of the demands of the moment. They share their understanding of theology, be it ever so minimal, and their knowledge of the world, be it ever so pressing. With a sincere effort to find God's will, and with the presence of God's Spirit to give them utterance, the group becomes as significant a medium for theological dialogue as Christendom can produce.

In the second place, learning among Christians is the residue of countless unplanned encounters and events. Regardless of the difference in age, intelligence, or experience, the dynamics of such encounters are the same. The young are nurtured into love through contact with the feeling tone of the community, through the reaction of adults when their limits are tested, through the degree they feel involved in the network of communication about them.

For the mature, enlightenment is a natural consequence of the spirit of the community. There is no embarrassment surrounding ignorance. It is expected and listened to. No one expects answers to come quickly, if they come at all. Christians can talk to one another in confidence because they know they will always need to tolerate some darkness, some immaturity, and therefore have a constant reason why they need one another to grow.

Edifying. This term will be a little difficult to distinguish from nurturing, for it also implies a building up, a development of spirit, a maintenance of the spirit of love among people; but the New Testament church apparently made a very marked distinction between the two. Edifying carries with it the overtone of affirmation, approval, and strengthening. "Let each of us please his neighbor for his good, to edify him." (Rom. 15:2.) It carries the meaning of support, underpinning, and of mutual firming up of the bulwarks of faith against forces that would tear it down. "Encourage one another and build one another up." (I Thess. 5:11.) Of course, the early church was in a position where this kind of support was exceedingly necessary, for Christians could not meet together without the knowledge that when they had finished their meeting they had to face a hostile and unchristian world. When the early church met, the members needed to draw from one another deep comfort and assurance. Christians today are faced with a similar, yet different, danger. We do not find it too hard to face the world. In fact, it is too easy, and our need for edification grows out of the fear lest our witness be lost in a friendly, cordial society.

How do Christians edify one another? By those means which develop a feeling of oneness, which is the natural consequence of a prior feeling of personal integrity in human relationship. The person who feels free enough to act out his life on his own terms in the presence of another is then ready to assume responsibility for acting out his life in terms of the other. However mysterious it seems, and in spite of its resistance to objective study and measurement, there is a level of communication where *the other one becomes me.* After prolonged association with the Christian community, the single Christian can not only affirm his membership in the fellowship, but can with equal assurance affirm that he bears about in his life something of the community.

As though to guarantee the maintenance of this embodiment of the fellowship in the person, the church directs its first effort toward common worship. When people sing, pray, listen, and dedicate their lives together week after week, something of the oneness of the church is bound to be built into the Christian. His common act of praise to God in the midst of the world is the occasion for the feeling of "commonness," which is a condition of the single Christian "plurality," or the answer to Christ's prayer that we might be one.

It should go without saying that here again, all casual or formal encounters with one another in the life of the church will determine the degree to which the Christians bear the church in their lives. Perhaps we are too impatient to accomplish goals in the church rather than in the Christian. Parliamentary procedure is necessary for an orderly movement of people toward their goals, but it should not be considered normative for the Christian fellowship. Some issues might be subjected to discussion, testimony, even prayer and fasting, not with the objective that they will pass by a majority vote, but rather that Christians will be in accord.

Common worship and common searching, plus prayers and support from fellow Christians will provide more than the knowledge that they are with me. I will know they are within me, that having grown through processes permitting me to be myself and to let myself be authenticated through the relationship of the other, I now stand not only authenticated by myself, but carrying with me the authentication from God revealed through his people. As the Christian community becomes internalized we are more and more apt to speak and act in terms of it.

Burden-bearing. Grief is the only burden people ever have to bear. The term has generally been used to define the feelings of one who has suffered loss through death, and of course, grief in its most intense sense probably is best understood as being the condition of the bereaved. On the other hand, any form of loss, failure, or tragedy carries an overtone of grief. Loss of job, loss of status, loss of friend, loss of self-respect, loss of social approval, loss of health, or loss of wealth are all occasions for grief.

Our question then becomes, how does the Christian talk to

another Christian who is in grief? What is done here is as little different from edifying as edifying is different from nurturing. Both move toward the involvement of one in the life of the other in acts and words of love. In grief, this is hardly changed, only intensified. We enter the life of the other one for the purpose of strengthening, of providing a " thereness " of ourselves. One of the most yearning desires of the person in grief is to have someone " there." And this means something more than simply being there in spirit. It means being there in body, being there to use voice, hands, and all other human facilities. It is the sort of communication that defies words. It is love made perfect in that we stand together in the presence of questions, the answers to which are known only to God. Thus the final and most significant act of communication within the Christian community almost does away with the familiar symbols of communication. Where there has been proper nurture and constant edification of one another, and when we come to the point of bearing the burden, however heavy, we accomplish what is probably the deepest form of communication known to Christians – and that is, having done all in this day, just to stand.

Chapter VI

The Gesture Toward the " Other "

With their own kind, Christians feel at home. We have mastered the language, thought, and structure of the Christian community, and, in general, have no difficulty negotiating the rites of passage into its membership. We enter the doors of the church with confidence and though we may not always be in agreement with its theology and program, we nonetheless feel comfortable in moving about within its environment. However, this is not the only kind of world in which we have to live. We must live in a world " other " than the church. We are at home here also. We know its laws, demands, and resources for making us comfortable. We have gained sufficient rapport with it to provide ourselves with a livelihood, and the world " other " than the church has become very meaningful to us. In this world, as in the church, we have to find places where we can feel at home.

The Nature of the " Other "

Every group of people large or small is an astounding interconnection and interpenetration of customs, ideas, words, beliefs, and symbols. Few individuals can understand and feel comfortable in all groups. We are selective, always searching for the groups and associations that are easily understood and where the symbols and customs are not threatening. If they do become threatening, we do one of two things. Either we stay in the group, become hostile, and resist the ideas and beliefs we do not understand or we run away. These who do the latter, in a large measure, must be considered as the " other." For people in our society there are a great many convenient avenues of departure from religious communities to groups where others " talk their language." The church is not strange to people outside. Probably more people than we think have had some contact with it, be it ever so brief. Most people know something about the church, even if only the location of a church building. At some time or other in their life they will undoubtedly seek its services to consecrate a child, bless a marriage, or perform the final ritual over the remains of the dead. Moreover, the church is ever pressing in upon all people in our society. It stands on the street corner, its ministry reaches into the educational, sociological, and economic concerns of our society, so that when the Christian bears his witness into the world he is not carrying it to people who need to hear the first word about the Christian way.

What are people like in the world outside the church? To begin with, they are very much like the Christian who wants to bring a change into their lives. They look and act much the same. Whatever differences exist are rarely evident on the surface, for both are sustained by the same culture. Moreover, these are not purposeless people with wholly unworthy or unattainable goals. The person who attempts to further the Kingdom of God soon becomes aware that the people in the world are trying to further other kingdoms. Only the person of deep psychotic disturbance is without purpose. The rest of us are constantly trying to " arrive at something." Our purposes may be hidden, even from ourselves, but they motivate us nevertheless. The range of these purposes is amazing. Some are very personal and immediate, such as maintaining contact with reality by getting through each day's work without breaking down emotionally. Others are centered in broader context, such as getting children through adolesence, cleaning up the community, making money, gaining status, or getting to heaven. In this vast array of counterpurposes within which the Christian must communicate the gospel to the world outside, we are not addressing ourselves to open and receptive vessels. In spite of the few exceptions we know about, people generally are not waiting with open hearts to hear Christ's redeeming word. If they have unfulfilled desires and goals, they are certain that these can be reached by making more money, building cleaner communities, or attaining greater assurance of getting to heaven.

As a communicator of the good news, the Christian finds himself in a profound encounter with purposive people. It is his word against theirs, argument against argument, persuasion and counterpersuasion. This tug of war is complicated further by the fact that the purposes these people embrace are " good." They have been born into a cultural milieu that has stamped its approval upon such purposes and trains its young to strive after them. They have developed images and symbols of money-making (and hoarding), good deeds (one a day), and service to community and nation, which make them sound exceedingly praiseworthy. Furthermore, they are not necessarily inimical to the Christian faith and might well have been born out of it.

Another reason, then, why Christians are probably suffering from a reticence regarding their mission to the world lies in the fact that what the Christian traditionally has had to offer is now being offered better and more adequately by other agencies of our society. In the first century and in the time of Christ himself, the Christian had little competition in ministering to the soft areas of man's need. This is no longer true in our culture. The hospital cares for men's physical illness; social welfare and government, for his social and economic needs. When his deep emotions become disturbed, he has recourse to the psychiatric and counseling resources of the community. It is little wonder that we find many Christian people working in these areas and diligently carrying the message of human welfare to the world. Moreover, this satisfies the curious dilemma of the Christian " layman." He can communicate at the level of "task performance" and become competent as a worker, while at the same time he need not communicate at the level of "building and maintaining" the faith, a responsibility given to the professional religionist.

Here is the tragic splitting apart of the Christian message. One woman put it very clearly when she said: "I feel I am a religious person. I am active in my church and I try to train my children to be Christian. I have interests in the community as well. I am an officer in one community welfare agency and am on the board of two others. But you asked me whether I ever talk to people about the Christian faith. I would never *think* of it. It just is not done and when the group of people I associate with outside the church come up to this question we all rather agree to drop the subject before we get into an argument that will separate us." The fact that she emphasized the word "think" indicates the prevailing pattern Christians have developed regarding communicating the gospel. It has been suppressed out of consciousness. It does not become an active ingredient or stab our conscience. The very discomfort that accompanies any attempt to communicate as Christian with the world has made us want to forget that this might be one of the responsibilities we need to bear. Thus, this chapter and the next establish some principles for the Christian witness in the world.

The Levels of Encounter

To begin with, the Christian will need to take into account the many levels at which he engages his world in acts of communication. How realistic is it for a Christian to be certain he is witnessing to his faith in the world? Christian communication is going on around us all the time. Billboards, television, radio, newspapers, the very presence of the church spire itself, are always constant reminders that the church is in the world and ready to teach the world, if it is permitted. We are often only too willing to let such communication sensitize the world to its need for God and the church, and then rely upon "regular channels " to evangelize and educate those who are persuaded. For all its coverage and results, mass communication is hardly a substitute for the intimate one-to-one contact the Christian can make with the world. All mass efforts can be sensitive only to mass opinion, and the feelings of the individual are lost. Regardless of how effective it becomes to have a few stimulate the many, the basic work of carrying the gospel to the world will need to be done in the close, daily interaction of the Christian with the one next to him. Relatively few are going to assume a position in the church where they are professionally or semiprofessionally responsible for preaching, teaching, or otherwise communicating with the world, nor is it necessary for any person to think he needs such status to be Christian. It is amazing to discover that the communication of the faith need not require us to alter in the least the normal activity of our lives. We shall continue to work, play, and otherwise maintain association with the world. What is demanded is that our first and strongest impulses be directed toward Christian words and activities.

How do we go about this? How can we reach the unreached? How can we set up the lines of communication between ourselves and another whose thought patterns are alien to our own? How is this done, especially when the readiness for communication present in the Christian fellowship is missing? In the last chapter we saw how in the church the mutual edification and loving support given one to the other is based upon a fund of emotional information with which all participants are familiar. This is present in only one participant when we speak to the " other." He knows neither our words nor symbols, let alone our meanings. He is not ready with a response to our signals. He may be only remotely aware of the worship forms that edify, build, and maintain the fellowship of God's people. Moreover, the Christian himself will undoubtedly wish for more insight and skill. Our knowledge of the faith might be only slightly greater, or even less, than the one to whom we make a Christian gesture. We cannot wait to communicate with the world until we have mastered the art. We must train on the job. Communicating is coincident with Christianity. Andrew went *immediately* to tell Peter about Jesus – no "cultivation," no training. The very development of Christian insights depends upon our experiences of communicating our feelings about them. And of course, as we develop insight, our skills in communicating develop.

The Transfer of the Church's "Information"

The gesture toward the other can be made on three rather well defined levels, each containing levels of its own. They are not mutually exclusive, for in every interpersonal event communication takes place at every level, ranging from the verbal gesture to the deepest meaning. At the surface level and in the broadest sense of the term, Christian communication is the transference of information to the world, for Christianity itself is informative. It has something to tell. It is newsworthy. It is filled with a surprising number of important events for almost everyone. The very fact of Christianity itself is of tremendous importance to anyone who attempts to understand his world. No day passes but that Christianity does not make a statement, perform an act, dedicate a church, christen a child, or perform a duty in the community. Sooner or later, these facts will need to be told.

However, it is this very information that gets us into trouble. The accumulation of this information throughout the ages has left us with a tremendously large residue of doctrine and history, and because this has been so vast and difficult for most people, including Christians, to understand, it is often avoided. Every now and again someone suggests that if dogma were done away with altogether it would be much simpler to live within the Christian community and certainly much easier to communicate with those outside the fellowship. Let us admit this might be all too true and all of us at once confess the error of our ways. The professional Christian has not made it easy for the amateur (if this be a good designation) to communicate with the world about the faith. Even the most basic words have lost their original meanings and appear to be out of date or at least irrelevant for our day. Klaus von Bismarck has suggested that this is true even of some of the most important words of our Christian vocabulary. He says:

> A word like conversion for example has no longer about it any of the radiant luster of the deliverance that is experienced when a man turns to Christ. Instead, it is associated if not with the idea of painful self-exposures in which immoral things are brought to light, then with the excesses of mainly professional evangelists. Repentance seems far removed from the Messianic anticipatory joy that the purifying immersion of John the Baptist signified. We think of the fines or of the penalties imposed by a policeman or a teacher. Grace too has lost all meaning for many people. They know that grace is something good. The Word has not yet lost its illuminating power completely. There is a light shining over it as there was over the stable at Bethlehem. But men do not find the way there through that sign. It is no longer grasped that grace means the wiping out of our offenses by God with a generosity compared to which the pardoning of a murderer before his judge is nothing, that it operates in all of us through Jesus Christ. Faith is historical belief in the facts of salvation and the message of the Bible. Thus the Word has not yet completely lost its meaning. Through experience in human relationships, do you believe in me? I have faith in you. There remains at least a trace of the original sense of it. Sin has entirely ceased to be associated with God and is seen only in relation to a morally understood church or pastorate that seeks to take away from people the little pleasure they have. The prototype of the sinner is the man or woman who lives more or less frivolously. The fact that sin as a dangerous separation from God is found in its diabolical self-awareness among morally blameless men and women is never dreamed of.[47]

How these terms changed meaning is hard to determine. It is easy enough to blame their obscurity on the professional theologian who generally speaks not to the man on the street, but to his fellow professionals. He refines his wares in such a way that they will be quite clear to those who make theological discipline their stock in trade. The greater the refinement, the farther the nonprofessional falls behind. He spends little time developing a theology or trying to understand the theology of other people. The terms " sin," " faith," " repentance," " conversion," have meaning for him only in so far as he is able to observe their application to the people in familiar situations. Three things should be said about this difficulty we have with the language of our theology.

First, words always form a barrier among people who are in communication.[48] It is doubtful as to whether any word we utter at any given time is clearly understood in all its ramifications by those who hear it. Once we say a word, we have committed ourselves to more words, for they will be needed to clarify the word originally used. Most of the words we use are elaborations and extensions of prior words. This is the way we make ourselves clear. We readily accept this when we are talking to people about other than religious things. If they do not understand the words we use in describing our work, a game, or an incident, we do not hesitate to take them through the necessary explanation if we are describing something we saw, we do not feel at all embarrassed by using new and strange terminology and then describing what it means to us and what it has meant to the people from whom we learned it. We may not even worry a great deal if some of the words do not come out completely clear. If we were to discount communication among other people because our words were not totally clear, then all of us would become mute, for anything we said would fall short of complete clarity.

In the second place, our words are the children of tradition. In general, our techniques for functioning in the world change much more rapidly than the words we use to describe them. In the fields of law, medicine, and even business, in spite of streamlined techniques in performing the tasks of the trade, much that goes on is accompanied by unclear terminology.

Words that have been used over the years mean a great deal. It is felt that something will be lost if a term is lost, even though the function it describes no longer exists. There seems to be something very comforting and supporting in the terms we use in one another's presence, and it often appears that using terms that are familiar to us is far more important than using terms that accurately describe the thing we are talking about. None of us wants to admit that we particularly like the minister or Sunday school teacher to use a word we do not understand, even though this word might very clearly describe the thing that is being talked about. And rather than surrender our comforting understanding of one another to up-to-date speech, we will hold on to words that probably do not carry the full meaning of what is present.

It is strange, therefore, that in the Christian religion we should raise as much commotion as we do about the fact that our words are archaic. When we criticize the loss of meanings of these things we must also remember that when people hear such terms as " sin," " faith," " repentance," " conversion," they may not be able to describe what is meant by them. Yet without question most of them will be able to relate these terms in some way to the original meanings given by the church and the culture.

The third thing about the informative words of our religion is that, like almost all words in our vocabulary, they were originally used for the purpose of helping people. When we speak about the content of the religion being very difficult, and sometimes even harmful to people in the process of communication, we must remember that a term appeared in the vocabulary of the church only after it was made certain that the church would benefit by its being there. No matter how multisyllabled or unfamiliar the word, it can hardly be doubted that its original purpose was for the benefit of persons and the ultimate salvation of their lives. To be sure, the original meanings have often been perverted and distorted so that they do not mean what they meant originally. Nevertheless, if stated at a time and in a way that has meaning to a conversation, they can still bear a message of good to those who hear them.

Doctrine and Human Behavior

How, then, can the content of the Christian religion be used when we attempt to witness in the presence of another? It is difficult to lay down broad principles that will fit every situation, for certainly not all of us possess the same degree of sophistication about our dogma; nor do the things that have been presented in the present-day church as its doctrine always apply in every situation. However, the second level of communication with the world outside may give us some hint as to the way in which the content can be used. It is quite likely that no word spoken in "defense" of the faith has ever been used apart from a concomitant meaning in the behavior of people. None of the terms mentioned above by Von Bismarck is free from the involvement of human personality. Taken in its very broad sense, theology refers to the religious experiences that happen to people, and when we use the term "religious thought" we refer to what the theologian "thinks" about the religious experience someone has had. Moreover, such experience happens to all persons.

Even though a person may calculatingly refute and turn aside every Christian gesture made toward him, he is nonetheless involved in a pattern of theological behavior. He sins, he becomes converted, he goes through daily sessions of repentance with people around him. He demonstrates a particular order of faith, manifests kindness, and shows evidences of all the things about which theology is concerned. The arena for establishing contact with any person is already constructed by the fact that we embody the things theology talks about. In this arena every Christian, regardless of his level of understanding of the dogma of the church, has access to the content of his religion, and is able not only to demonstrate it in his own life, but to help people engage in an exploration of it. In a sense, it is at this point where theology itself is born, and presiding at its birth are not only (maybe even not usually) the professionals, but, as well, the nonprofessional people who stand by.

No Christian need make apology for his theology nor does he need any sort of blessing from the church to validate his witness. That the person is in possession of something that should be shared with others is a natural and ultimate consequence of being a Christian. These acts of " having and sharing " should in no way minimize the importance of eventually formulating theological ideas and structuring them in a logical pattern of explanation. But it cannot be overemphasized that theology does not have its beginning with this final formulation. Standing prior to every theological dogma that the church possesses is man's need and man's response to that need in terms of his search for God and God's revelation to him. This is precisely what Jesus was asking Peter on the mount when Peter was called upon to confess. (Matt., ch. 16.) Jesus was saying: What stands back of your relationship with me? Wherein have you understood me and what is it I mean to you in terms of the deep content of your life? Peter was not simply responding to a fulfillment of prophecy or to the normal development of Old Testament hope and belief. When he replied, he was saying that there is something here that fills my heart and this I must express. " You are the Christ, the Son of the living God."

The Level of Feeling

It well may be that all we can expect to do when talking with the " other " is to let our true feelings emerge. What fills our lives? What do we do with our guilt? Where is our peace? However, we do not just go up to people and let answers to these questions come rushing out. Many Christians with insights fail to make them helpful simply because the communication system is inadequate. There are steps in this system that can give meaning to the relationships and assist in sharing insights. At the most basic level, it goes without saying that anyone who has need for forgiveness of sin does not fully understand the dynamics of his forgiveness. Moreover, a great many people have been turned to God, have had a renewed vision for their lives, and have been given a new understanding of purposes for their lives without having understood at all what was happening to them. They might not have known there could be an explanation. This does not mean, however, that it is not possible for them to understand. The process by which people learn is exceedingly slow and subtle. To give logical form to our attitudes and feelings is not a simple process for anyone, and for some it may be impossible.

It is precisely at this point that our Christian education methods need examination. We tend to treat all as though they were at the same level of religious experience. Any form of mass education must suffer under this necessity, but it is especially damaging when it happens in areas where feelings and attitudes are important. When persons who may be well matured in the ways of the world and have found complete adjustment in countless group relationships come to religion, they are quite inadequate and are as children. The early church recognized this. Paul, when he talked about "childhood" and "maturity," was hardly thinking of children in a chronological sense, but rather in a spiritual sense. (See especially I Cor. 14:20; Gal. 4:3; Eph. 4:14.) The child has feelings long before he can translate those feelings into concepts. The child is educated by these feelings and it will be a long time until what is happening to him can be logically understood. Logical understanding may never happen, and certainly it should not happen to anyone if, in the process, he should lose the feeling tones and insights of Christian love. Thus it is with our approach to those outside the church. If we approach them immediately with the full weight of theological dogma, we offer them things that cannot be handled within their frame of understanding.

Within the framework of the church, a great many people, especially children, are always in this status of translating feelings into beliefs and understanding at the rational level. In fact, most church school teachers are occupied most of the time with presiding at such a translation, whereby spiritual understanding moves from elementary and unreasoned insights to the more complex logical interpretations that are available. In a sense, then, the church is speaking to the " world " when it teaches the small child who, through the educational enterprise, is growing in the fellowship. The child's feelings about religion are simple. He needs simple identification with stories in the Bible, stories of the early church and of the church's development, stories of good works, and the feeling that children have for others who are engaged in behavior they can understand.

A problem arises in that the teacher is never free from the temptation to hurry the person from the level of feeling to the level of dogma. His own formulations are a necessary part of his " intrusion " as a teacher, and he will want to employ them. However, something of his own maturity can be understood in the way he persists in pushing doctrine ahead of feeling. If, in the Christian's own life, the feelings of love and concern have been taken over by " beliefs " about them, it is only on the basis of these beliefs that he can communicate. His orientation in belief will encourage him to talk rather than listen. He presses for affirmation of his beliefs, for dogma without life insists upon its own way. Love, with or without dogma, insists upon the way of God in the dialogue. It is this feeling, this identification of person with person, this movement of love, the willingness of a person to stand with another under the judgment of God's Spirit, which is primary and basic in all of our witnessing. If it is necessary to move to this other level of formulating these feelings in terms of the dogma and checking it against the history of the church, it is only because this witnessing needs to continue and communication of the faith must never stop. Mood precedes doctrine, and in this pattern the Christian confronts his world, whether it be the child growing into the church, or the adult on the outside.

The Level of Language

There is a third level of communication with the world that may even precede the step just mentioned. Prior to the theological feeling tones, the gesture toward the other must begin where the Christian and the world understand a mutual language. It is sometimes difficult to establish a relationship on the basis of experience and feeling. Most of us have had the experience at one time or other of returning after many years' absence to a high school or college class reunion. We enthusiastically greet a friend we knew well in school, but after the initial small talk and pleasantries, we suddenly find he is engaged in very little with which we have anything in common. Conversation slows down. He is of a different political party, and a different religion. In college or high school this made little difference, but now they separate us. The kind of work he does is foreign to us, his home environment and his community life are something we neither know nor understand. Although for three minutes we are quite exuberant in each other's presence, soon we have said everything that can be said, not only because we do not understand the things each other is doing, but also because we do not have any depth of feeling level on which to function.

The language is strange because experiences are different. This is one of the reasons why those who witness " at random " in our world are apt to find that their results are meager or superficial. It is only after we have engaged the " other " in closeness and friendship that it is possible to begin the gesture toward him. This is the basic, primary relationship through which the person skillfully wins his way into the confidence of the " other." His ultimate goal is to make his association with these persons satisfy all the basic elements in the communication " event " – the needs and integrity of the persons involved and the claims of the gospel of Jesus Christ.

This does not necessarily mean that we have to compromise or become like the other person. The most satisfying aspects of relationships are not always the things that can be designated as pleasurable or even happy. Any relationship can be said to be satisfying only when its words and acts move the participants toward education and healing. The end result of some encounters may be frustration, conviction, guilt, or feelings of failure. If we are sincere in winning our way into the life of another, he will sense that our need to be with him is not simply for the purposes of self-gratification, but to share in a common quest. Both persons can then tolerate failure and doubt. Having answers is secondary to having the feeling of close association with one whose only motivation is to love.

All of us are entitled to the experience of deep friendship. Carlyle and Chesterfield used to meet every week and do nothing but sit together in silence; when they parted, they thanked each other for a pleasant conversation. Whether by silence or words, understanding comes because in the presence of one another we have the feeling that there are satisfying results being obtained and the association ought to be continued and renewed. The Christian can easily be tempted to circumvent the task of establishing closeness, and substitute a bag of tricks, or a mien of self-righteousness and high-pressure tactics. If he has a prepared speech or has developed little ways of getting at people, or carries convenient little tracts and other promotional schemes to forward the work of the Kingdom, he feels a certain competence in the cause he represents. He immediately establishes the fact that he is of a different world. He is asking people to engage in a dialogue designed to test theories, rather than inviting them into a redemptive encounter. The latter must always be the first gesture toward the world. One wonders whether outsiders, when confronted by such overorganized ways of witnessing to the gospel, are not repelled by them.

This will mean, of course, that any gesture toward the world will have to be made on the basis of a knowledge of the world and in constant relationship with it. Jesus himself warned and instructed his disciples about this very kind of relationship with people. In his last prayer he prayed that they might not be taken from the world, but remain in it. (John, ch. 17.) Remaining in it, however, they were not necessarily to become a part of it or to let it dominate them. The world can so easily overcome the Christian, for he has a great deal at stake in it. He makes his living there, and he needs to prove himself an acceptable member of the secular community. Therefore, in order to witness to the faith of his Christian convictions he will run into minor resistances and difficult situations where he feels forced to relegate his convictions to a secondary place. Yet stay in the world he must, at any cost.

Learning the Language of the " Other "

If we are going to communicate with the world of the " other " effectively, we shall need to learn its language. This may not be so difficult as it appears on the surface because in our relationship with other people our words almost automatically adapt to the mood we sense in the other. Notice how many people " talk down " to children by framing words and sentences as they see the children expressing them. When we speak to the sick, we automatically do so in sober and sometimes morbid tones. Most of us fall prey to conformity and equalization at this point. We almost instinctively know what kinds of words to use and how loud to speak them in specific situations. Of course there is a danger in this, the same danger that is present in any attempt to conform to the world. It is the danger that we shall speak this language and readily forget the language of the faith that lies deepest in our hearts, the language of love, of patience and kindness, of long-suffering and mercy, and of our own integrity. The child needs the adult in us, the sick need our health, the weak can use our strength.

In spite of the danger, using the language of the other person is elementary in establishing contact with him. There is something built into us that always wants to reach for another, especially if he attracts us, and the Christian ought to have a great many people who attract him. Unfortunately, the person who goes out in the name of his Christian belief often is resistant to this form of language-learning. He has the language, the only language, and it must be defended. Studies are being made now to determine whether the learning of language itself may have some relation to our feelings about people. Whatever these studies will show, it certainly makes some sense to believe that if there is a " blocking "of feeling and concern for the person, this blocking will eventually be betrayed at the level of speech.

But the true Christian is not like this. His understanding of what is in his heart tells him how he must approach others. It makes him want to learn the " way " of the other, to see his point of view, stand where he stands, to let him speak, learn of his life, and to know more about him in any given situation than he knows about himself. Such attentiveness is bound to shift the focus of the event from *what God has done for me* to *what God can do in our midst.* The danger is not in telling what happened to us. The danger rather comes in that the language we use in telling what happens to us is not accurately symbolic of what has taken place in our lives. The Christian can justifiably speak only the words that describe what is taking place in the encounter. Otherwise, there is no understanding, and communication stops. To be sure, all people must speak out of past experiences; but for the Christian, the past is gathered into the immediate circumstance, and he wants only to provide an arena where the Holy Spirit can judge and instruct.

Sometime ago a friend of mine was called upon to arbitrate a labor-management dispute in the town where he was serving as a minister. When the labor group heard of the appointment, they objected strenuously on the grounds that a minister in this discussion would be a handicap. They said the meetings would be unrestrained and the group would be giving full rein to language that the minister would hardly approve. The minister was prepared for this, and the answer he gave was one of the reasons why he was able to remain in the relationship.

The minister replied that it did not make much difference what language was used. What did make a difference was that everyone should understand one another.

Maintenance of Integrity

One of the most difficult things for sincere Christians to do is to permit others to be themselves in the initial relationships, and at the same time to maintain their own integrity. We have spent much of our time educating Christians to agree and be agreeable, and too little time teaching them what to do in situations where lack of agreement is both inevitable and obvious. In the major communication areas, it is possible to plan for smooth movement of signal and response. Mass media in particular work so close to the level of "perfection" in pleasing the eye and ear, that one "fluff" can constitute a near-tragedy. Planning, rehearsal, and evaluation of listener and reader response can produce almost infallible techniques of "reaching" people. The objective is to shorten the distance between signal and response, and eliminate search for meaning or discussion of whether a product is as good as it is claimed to be. (Even the mass media assume that the listener looks for meaning, hence commercials are loaded with considerable evidence that someone else has answered the question of meaning: "Laboratory tests prove . . ." or, "A well-known testing service has shown . . .")

Would it be too critical to look in the same direction at some of the techniques of making the Christian gesture toward the world? Does the desire for smoothness and order suppress meaning? When we learn how to knock on a door, get the television set turned off, bring the whole family into a mood of listening, and even presuppose certain questions by having answers to the "standard" objections to the intrusion of the church, we are setting the scene for agreement and harmony.

It seems reasonable that the Christian will eventually reach a point of moral, ethical, or theological impasse in his conversation with the world. When we go to the non-Christian, we are dealing with an " adversary," albeit not in the sense of his being a hostile enemy plotting to overthrow us. He is " other," however, in that he places the need for spiritual orientation of his life at a level lower than Christian. At some point in the Christian and non-Christian dialogue the level will be unmasked. It may emerge at the point of morals where we will be mildly shocked, or in a brand of ethics completely contradictory to the Christian gospel. What does a Christian do when the non-Christian comes up with horrifying ideas about heaven, hell, or the incarnation?

Our best answer, of course, is Jesus' answer, " Do not be anxious," even if the adversary becomes hostile and wants to drag one before judges. (Matt. 6:25 ff.) Anxiety has a way of driving us either to the shelter of words and counterattack, or back into the comfort of the fellowship where we are " free from all alarm." What does it mean to to be " unanxious "? We do not have from Jesus an attribute to replace anxiety, but one gets the impression that it would be something akin to faith. What then is the meaning of faith in our communication with the world?

Faith is the assurance of the integrity of our undergirding Christian love and the accompanying confidence that God is present in all human events. The resulting mood is one of " high neutrality," or a mood of patient attentiveness. This may be all a Christian can do when there is a gulf between him and another. Persuasion will accomplish little and compromise will accomplish less. When we overcome the temptation to persuade or compromise (the fruits of anxiety), God will direct us to the alternative. He will help us to understand, to wait for more meaning and deeper insight, and for the moment we may simply have to say, " I suppose we are not together."

The Christian is always performing the loving act when he is tentative and accepting. Nothing should be surprising to him, however distasteful or sinful the situation may seem. One of the marks of Jesus was that he seemed to maintain his individuality under all conditions. He was at home almost anywhere. This art of being a universal person is not easily learned, for it is anxiety-creating, and with ease we pull back into the groups where our language is understood, and where we can easily receive the signals sent out by others. For all its universality, the church will need to admit that it shows serious weakness in communicating with groups whose " world mien " is foreign to it. Manual laborers, the hosts of migrant workers, the very rich and the very poor, those who inhabit the world of crime and near-crime, certain types of the sick, the mentally ill, and others in our community whose ways are often foreign to ours, are not easily reached because of the span of language that has to be crossed before communication can be established.

Qualifications for Confronting the World

The good communicator, then, becomes a sounding board. In every situation he listens for the language of the other. He listens for the overtones of need, the cultural expectancies, and then adapts himself. He is not merely a silent partner in this, for a sounding board is a reflecting, responding, and returning agent. People want our understanding and our acceptance more than they need our advice. To be a good listener requires a faith that God has made all men to hear his Spirit within their lives. We should not attempt to give people what God can give them in greater degree and quality. Whether a man turns from his selfishness and pride to a life of love and kindness is ultimately a matter between God and himself. We stand as a participant in this quest having concern for his condition as well as needs of our own that are being met in the process.

How simple it would be if we could answer the religious needs of people merely by listing the formulas and reciting the creeds of the church. Indeed it is precisely this which only too often we attempt to do. When ministers are asked to lead in prayer, when Christians are asked to participate in public functions, when we make any endeavor to display our wares as Christians before people, it is generally with a verbalizing of those things which are *our* language. The other person becomes silent and respectful, but not does respond, simply because he cannot understand and because the cost of building the bridge from himself to the church is too great and he needs someone to help.

Each day we meet people functioning at all three of the levels we have stated here. We meet with those for whom the idea of Christian love and feeling, let alone the content of the Christian faith, is completely strange or nearly so. All we can do is attempt to get into their lives, learn their language, understand them when they speak, and learn to move within their orbit, while maintaining the integrity of our own Christian convictions and insights. We also meet people who have felt something of the nature of Christian understanding and love. They come to sense their status before God. They are raising the ultimate questions of life. With such we must continue this quest. Still others are in the process of developing new insights concerning the content of the faith.

Therefore the Christian is a versatile person. The world is his. He knows no group or situation in which he does not have some clue to its improvement. He can truly become all things to all men; and when we speak of all men this means persons *as they are.* We harbor a dream that men shall be saved, and we like to think of them in this way. In looking at people " for what they can become " we are apt to seek out those who give the best promise of becoming, and look for communication with the " high potential " persons. Certainly we cannot know everything about all conditions that men have to face. We may not know what it is to be desperately ill, mentally or physically. We may not know the meaning of abject poverty or tragedy, yet the loving Christian has a facility for seeing the person, any person, as a self. Within his life, the Christian is " all men," a world man, who gives not only himself, but shares with others something of themselves. With this gesture he is reaching toward the other.

To perform on these three levels, the Christian must look at himself and his task in terms of at least four specific qualities of his relationship with other people. In the first place, the Christian can function only partly if he is not possessed with a passion for people and the condition of their souls. Without this, the whole subject of communicating as a Christian is utterly superfluous, for the one characteristic of the Christian faith is that there is an undying desire to make a gesture toward others. The manifestations of this quality we may disdain in some persons, but it is not because the quality itself is of no value. It is rather that the quality as they demonstrate it is gravely misused. The deepest form of Christian witness can take place only when affection and personal involvement occur in the direction of the "other." It is the one enduring power we have. Ordway Tead, in his book *The Art of Leadership* says:

> The power of the person is the *passion* of the person. It is the passion for truth which marks the important philosopher or teacher. It is the passion for righteousness which makes the great moral leader. (It is not) without significance in this connection that passion means in its original sense the capacity to suffer and endure.[49]

One would normally think that with all the scare headlines and the threat of the world's becoming increasingly involved in its own tyranny, centering itself upon its own destruction, men would rise up and the Christian would become highly sensitized to his need to proclaim this answer to the world's problems. But no such thing seems to occur. Maybe because we have so long stayed away from the communicating process at the deepest levels of our concern we have gradually lost the passion which gave birth to the church and with which it has been sustained throughout history. But the acquisition of this is a highly personal affair. It cannot be legislated; it cannot ultimately be taken out of another; it cannot be given by another. Finally each man stands before God and finds it for himself.

Second, it is also to be expected that the Christian will know something about his faith, and will have access to resources by which he can verify the things he is feeling. One of the marks of the Christian is his capacity to improve his skill in building a " reason " for the faith that is in him. The presence of the sustaining belief system provides a constant enthusiasm, which beyond a certain point cannot be " faked." Adherence to the Christian faith on any basis other than deep personal commitment will eventually be a block to the communication of that faith and turn enthusiasm into a compulsion whose origin we may not recognize.

The confrontation the Christian makes with the world, therefore, must also be made within himself. He cannot escape the fact that he has never reached final ground in his pursuits. No theologian would ever be ready to admit that the final word has been spoken in terms of God. If it has, then God is not nearly so far off and so great and so wonderful as we say he is, because a God who can be understood fully by the kinds of minds we seem to have is hardly God enough for us. But this does not keep us from having a faith and a central sustaining belief system that provides a faith, albeit growing and constantly changing. As it changes we should be willing to change with it. As our love deepens, our understanding of what is happening to us deepens. And as our understanding of what is happening to us deepens, then we have made the conditions in which love itself can deepen again. Thus man is never quite free from this circular behavior within his life wherein the poles of sheer content on the one hand and feelings of love, mercy, and fruits of the spirit on the other are ever lifting him to higher levels of insight. Furthermore, this intellectual activity keeps a rein upon the passion we feel for others. Our work in the world becomes meaningful and our endeavors to reach other people are not filled with undirected and unmeaningful activity.

Third, belief and passion develop purpose. We become selective within our environment. We are not random in our approach to the world. We set a direction which is planned and reasoned. We can establish priority in the use of our energies. We know the persons with whom our witness will be most effective. Often this is ill-defined. Even in the church where we have prided ourselves on the way in which we can organize our evangelism and our programs of education we often leave to chance the things that ought to be purposive. The church school teacher will prepare a lesson for "everyone." The minister prepares a sermon for "everyone." When we go out to visit the people there is only the most casual care taken to make certain that the persons to whom we go are the ones with whom the degree of readiness has been calculated beforehand.

Finally, these three foregoing qualities of our lives will form the level and strength of our gesture to the "other." It is our surface tension that gives people their first introduction to us. Our lives are like newspapers. Our first gesture is like the headlines that tell the whole story to many people, regardless of what they read underneath. Our initial purposes and direction will color everything that is said afterward. If we are not discriminating in our relationship with others, or if our passion carries us away and we appear to be "on fire for God," some people are apt to get "burned up." Regardless of how sincere we are and regardless of how in our inner lives we have reconciled all these facts for ourselves, it will nonetheless prove true that the persons will be known to us and we to them by the degree of energy and relationship we manifest on the surface when we talk with them.

Our purposes, belief systems, and underlying passions will evidence themselves in the body movement, ease of speech, and other simple aspects of our life style, which are a part of the communicating process itself. Our gestures, words, level of tone, degree of ease, and every other form of communication that human life can muster, will have its origin in these other three. This makes it important to maintain our own faith at a high level of sensitivity. Personality exists in a " field." We are not isolated individuals but participants in a " situation as a whole." The boundaries of the " situation as a whole " are indeterminate and it is across these vague and shifting " lines " that we speak to people. There is something deep in man which provides a subtle transfer of feelings and thoughts. Although we know very little about extrasensory communication in man, we are aware of the direct subconscious relationships that take place among people. It is this very type of transfer that is present whenever we address ourselves to the " other," and no matter how many variations of technique and communication we employ, the final validation of our success as Christian people in the world will be whether or not we have established contact at the deepest and most significant level of personal life, which is in God, from him, and at his direction.

Chapter VII

Authority in the Raised Question

In describing the communication of the gospel as a process characterized by the language of love and patience, do we not introduce into this dominant and ruling way of life a note of uncertainty? Should we not be more final, absolute, and authoritative? Moreover, does not such an uncertain relationship rob the person of his need to find a center around which he can develop a faith, and a language about it? In a world where all forms of human interaction are fraught with tentative and ambiguous meaning (" If the bugle gives an indistinct sound, who will get ready for battle? " [I Cor. 14:8]), will the gospel be known through the Christian whose method of encounter appears to be indefinite, and sometimes even stumbling or contradictory?

Communication and Authority

In spite of our emotional need for uncertainty, and our resistance to uncertain proclamations of our faith, the term " authority " has fallen upon hard times. It has been associated with prejudiced and rigid methods of dominating others. Recent trends in Christian education, group leadership, and teaching methods generally have aimed at the reduction of authoritarian techniques. In so doing, some important things have had to suffer. In the first place, authority itself has suffered. Since it is despised, no one wants to be associated with it. It is the subject of widespread condemnation. It floats free, and is therefore vulnerable to seizure by persons, both great and small, who use it for their own purposes.

Secondly, and more significantly, the Christian's image of himself as a communicator suffers. The church school teacher feels an uncertain status. The church official finds his satisfaction in administration, organization, and promotion. The request to issue a statement of faith along with his statement of the condition of the treasury would be anxiety-creating. Christians in general will be silent about their faith in the episodes of daily living rather than risk communicating a faith of which they cannot be certain.

Thirdly, it is the communication of the gospel itself which has suffered most. If the Christian keeps silent, the witness is lost. The responsibility for this loss must be borne, in large measure, by the church, which has not kept alive a clear and constant evaluation of the authority by which it speaks. Moreover, the concepts of authority prevalent in the church have, in general, been carried over from the culture and endowed with religious meanings. It appeals to belief, creed, status, and tradition, and appears to be what Ruesch and Bateson have called a "functional authority."[50] It is authority based upon superior knowledge and advantageous position. They point out that in American education this type of authority is checked by eager students who raise questions and demand objective evidence. Although the church is gradually moving toward such question-asking (group processes are shaking us loose), what actually takes place in its preaching, teaching, and personal witness still looks like Ruesch and Bateson's description of the authoritarian teacher in Europe. He is the unquestioned authority, and carries on his work through an exhibition of his knowledge, which is beyond and safe from all questioning.

With an attitude toward authority that ranges from disdain to disregard, we should not be surprised that our communication of the gospel will be carried on either as undisciplined sentimentality or unsentimental persuasion. Are these the only alternatives? To begin with, it should be recognized that as mature Christians, we live and act on the basis of something we can rightly claim as the spiritual authority for our lives. From their earliest years we have learned to draw personal meaning from the concepts of life, death, God's will, the meaning of Christ, and the requirements for our salvation. It is only natural that these should be held with unwavering faith. God is at work in us, and so strong have these meanings become that they "possess" us. They are the will of God; so, in truth, God possesses us.

On the other hand, as soon as persons feel they are possessed by something, they usually counter by taking possession. When the Christian feels "laid hold upon by God," he assumes he can improve his position by "laying hold" of God. God is the "property" of the Christian, and therefore he feels free to extend "it" toward others or, if necessary, force "it" upon them. Since these beliefs hold us together, we invest much time and effort holding them together. Not being equally certain at all points regarding our beliefs, we search for more certainty and clearer explication. To accomplish this we study, either alone or in the church community where others share in the constant reinforcement of the belief patterns. Sooner or later, however, we will use a convenient method to validate and strengthen our inner selves. We will use other people by asking them to listen to us as we talk about the way we think and believe. If, in this process, we can bring them to believe as we do, our position needs no further authentication. There is nothing quite so convincing in our lives as having someone share our position, even if we need to employ argument and other forms of persuasion.

These two aspects of authority – the need for it and the need to affirm it – usually result in the type of education and communication wherein the minister "proclaims," the teacher "teaches," and the Christian "witnesses." Often the more unclear the issues, the more proclaiming, teaching, and witnessing. The importance of certainty carries the person into the events of communication with such a momentum of certainty-seeking that he becomes authoritarian, and immediately the very concepts that hold him together become a liability in human encounter.

Authority Derived from the Nature of the Gospel

No matter how certain, how authentic, how rewarding the gospel is to us, when we come to share it with others, a whole new set of principles is required. What is certain and affirmable in the person becomes tentative and experimental when he relates to another. In the encounter, a new level of relationship begins to function. It is not built upon years of refinement and reinforcement. It does not have the advantage of a coherent and working belief system. No matter how close two people may be, they develop their personal faith independently. Even if both are Christians, the difference in their supporting belief systems may be great. If one of them is not Christian, the difference can be amazing. What stands within persons does not necessarily stand between them, for here is virgin territory, an area of young and tender development. Here is where the "communication of" meets the demands of "communication between." [51] The living, vital message must come under the demands of the "telling." Let us suppose the Christian is committed to the Christian way, and also wants to share it with others. Assuming he cannot launch his ideas and beliefs indiscriminately, he will need to ask what principle governs the sharing process.

The principle is derived from the nature of the gospel itself. In matters of communication, the church and its people have been borrowers. Methods of doing almost anything in the church generally have been tested first under nonchurch auspices. Education in the church follows the lead of secular systems whose fundamental reasons for existence may be entirely different. To promote its life and raise its funds, the church draws heavily from the world of secular education, industry, and commerce. It need not be argued that techniques used by other groups might well apply to the church, but the point remains that because it can obtain its techniques ready-made, it seldom inquires whether there is anything inherent in the gospel itself which establishes guidelines for the techniques of communication.

F. W. Dillistone[52] has suggested that, for the purpose of its communication, the gospel is both a story and a picture – the story of the activities of Jesus of Nazareth, and a picture of a central figure whose life turns about one burning center, the place of death and resurrection. These form a model for the integration of the universe, and a disclosure of the will of God to men. In one form or another, these aspects have always been ground for an overview of the meaning of the Christian faith. It would seem, however, that a third aspect cannot be overlooked. The gospel has to do with the way it passes from person to person. It is the story *told*, the picture *painted*. It is not only news, but the method of carrying the news. When the Christian enters an event with another, he is not only the bearer of the message but, as well, the " way " of the message. Is not this what Jesus meant by his being the " Way "? He went about things the " way " we should go about things. The gospel is the " way " we meet and address one another, and the " way " the good news is extended to the world.

Christian Encounter as Exploration

Christian communication, then, is always an exploratory event, and as such, must take on the characteristics of exploration. Being a " look around " animal, man carries on this search mainly with his eyes. Because of our amazing interest in ourselves and things around us, we use our eyes to make ourselves comfortable in our world. We have developed a remarkable capacity for sizing things up. We look for " our own," the things and people that annoy us least, and can enhance our pleasure and comfort. Our lives are spent constructing paths in which we can walk with the least amount of disturbance. This process is sometimes called "canalization."[53] Like many words in our vocabulary, it is descriptive of its meaning. It suggests a canal that restricts traffic to a particular path. We sample our environment, trying out various responses on a trial-and-error basis. When satisfying results are found, we maintain them. Eventually, this accounts for our love of the customary order of things. We live with, talk to, and associate with people who are like us. They are comforting folks; they do not beg for our money, or ask us to spend our time in unpleasant ways. They have no chance to mock us or riddle our conscience with the bombardment of their cries for help. They are our fortress, the *entrez-nous* group who speak our language and share our points of view.

To keep in touch with his world, the Christian will need to broaden his spectrum of interest. It moves out of its fixed ways and finds places it can be effective. This is the first movement of communication. It is the seeking, searching, exploring act. It should not be indiscriminate nor random. For each person, all other people maintain a social "distance." Some are very close, others are within reach, and still others are farther away, extending to the millions in the world the average Christian will never see. Our first question then is at what point we focus our attention. Who are the persons most likely to respond to our invitation to encounter and conversation? Who will hear us and feel our influence? When one dares to lift his eyes beyond the familiar religious arena, he becomes aware of an amazing number of areas of his life never touched by the question of religion. He discovers a great facility for wide swings of religious interest in his life. He can pull himself abruptly away from a week's work, play, and the activities associated with "living," come and participate in a highly concentrated form of religious observance and education, and just as abruptly re-enter the world of "other than religion."

The process should be more stable. To be sure, one cannot constantly maintain a high level of witnessing at all times.

We cannot always be a "missionary" by conscious attention. However, the tenets of love suggest that one's presence in the world should be *invitational and bidding*. The Christian is an "open" person. He is aware of the subtle signs that indicate the degree of readiness which is basic for any relationship. The subverbal language of the eyes, body, and gesture tells us much even before words are uttered. Some people are very active. They never seem to be relaxed, and give the impression they are always getting ready to go somewhere. These "motor types" will react much differently from the reserved, expressionless, noncommunicative person, or the person who is extremely outgoing, verbal, positive, and strong. Each one of these persons is acting just as he has learned to handle his relationships with other people. This is the way *he* feels comfortable, and generally he will relate to everyone the same way.

Moreover, the same person may have learned to handle himself by varying moods. In the presence of some people (especially those "over" him), he may be docile, accepting, and very co-operative. At another time (when relating to those "under" him), he might be outgoing, aggressive, and even harsh. This means, of course, that this same person will respond to another depending upon the way he interprets the relationship. Generally speaking, before the person to whom we turn can solve the problems of Christian thought, he will need to solve the problem of being in our presence. Because of this, the Christian may well be temporarily baffled by people. This is likely the most prevalent reason for shielding our religious witness from the world. It is not that we lack personal belief or feel inadequate concerning the content of our religious faith. It is rather that we distrust our capacity to relate to others. Realizing how charged religion is with emotion, rather than risk the security of our relationship with people we prefer to stay away from the subjects which might easily unsettle that relationship.

The difference in personal characteristics might be handled

in another way. Recognizing the differences, we might assume that in things religious we are dealing with an area transcendent to normal personal behavior, and adopt a single technique that is used on everyone, regardless of his readiness or his personality make-up. This singleness of process usually takes on the characteristics of one of two types of directness.

The first is unqualified directness. Many people encounter others with the same kind of certainty and straightforwardness that characterizes their personal beliefs. They move directly into the lives of other people. They have a message and an urgency about proclaiming it. They are concerned that the story of the gospel be told. Little or no attempt is made to build a relationship with the person to whom the message is directed, or to evaluate the readiness of the person to hear. Since we have learned that such procedures produce few lasting results, it is only the rare group or individual who follows such uncontrolled methods.

The second is subtle directness. The vast majority of Christians recognize the variables, and individual differences present in all forms of human interaction. They and the church at large have developed all sorts of schemes to soften the impact of the gospel. The initial assumption that the message must be told directly does not change. What is in the heart and mind one must get into the heart and mind of another. And so psychological trickery often becomes a substitute for the loving gesture. Rewards are offered, punishment is promised, and appeals to the emotions are made to motivate others to "see things our way."

The Bidding Approach

It has somehow been presumed that the only alternative to a direct approach to people are permissive techniques that seem to aim toward removing the communicator from the scene altogether. It is hoped that by minimizing the "teacher" in a situation, the person will pull from himself the answers to his questions. Of course the teacher's need to assist in this process is recognized, but in the main his part has been minimized. It is generally not perceived that if a society is to continue and Christian values are to be kept alive, it will be necessary for persons to intrude into the lives of one another. A continuous process of stimulation and counterstimulation is at work whenever people meet. Parents intrude into the lives of their children, mates sensitize each other, friend stimulates friend, and certainly the teacher moves significantly into the lives of the learners.

Although our personal patterns of belief and faith must remain intact, it is precisely from these that our Christian witness arises. It is with these that we make our intrusion. Somehow or other, in every situation we have the responsibility for introducing the relevance of the Christian gospel. It does not proceed by an elucidation of "all that Christ means to me," nor does it expect the burden of the relationship to be borne by the other. When people meet, something is structured "among them." Even though each of them has developed a "way of life," what exists between them may not be developed at all. In such a situation, the Christian introduces the gospel not merely as his "way of life," but *as the way the encounter should proceed.*

It cannot be assumed that what is most clear to us is clear to others. It is a sign of unsureness when persons or groups of persons want to deliver themselves immediately of all they think and believe. It is a sign of Christian love when the mood of encounter is the mood of seeking. We forget that

> Once I was a seeker;
> I sought both night and day.

Since we have "found," we like to think that others are seekers also, and that we have the responsibility for making their pilgrimage for them. Since most people are not consciously seeking the thing we have found, and since it is impossible for us to do their finding for them, we must search for another ground for our communication.

This area of witnessing is "between" persons. In this tender, emerging area of relationship the authority for communicating the gospel lies. It is not man's authority, it is God's authority; the authority of the presence of his Spirit. In the presence of this Spirit we are on a quest with another who shares this relationship and it is only because of the presence of God's Spirit that we can communicate it at all. It stands between us. It is the judge, the enlightener, the love-giving factor in the encounter that will make all the difference in the world as to whether the gospel of Jesus Christ is to be proclaimed or remain nothing more than a comforting adjunct of our own lives. When we speak to another, we not only bid his presence with us, but, as well, we bid the presence of the Spirit of God. And this loving, enlightening, seeking Spirit bids us both become involved in an event.

The Invitation to Give

The initial question in establishing a mood for God's authority is, "What have you to give me?" Learning how to receive is one of the more undeveloped aspects of Christian love. Most of us subscribe, tacitly at least, to the principle of giving as the highest form love can take, and giving implies our offering something that belongs to us. While it is true that Christianity has always emphasized this sort of giving, it is also true that Jesus himself and the witness of Christendom are on the side of a deeper, farther step in Christian love. Christian love reaches its highest expression when the loving one so structures a relationship that the other one is "given" the opportunity to give. It seems almost too much to be coincidence that in John's Gospel the words, "I thirst," were almost the last statement Christ uttered upon the cross. With these words he was opening his love to permit another to give something to him. Of course he was suffering the deep deprivation of body fluid, but his act assumes a deeper meaning when we see that he invited into his life the very persons who were putting him to death. He was inviting the person to give something of himself and thereby demonstrated the highest form of love. Christians so often want to give, and give again, that we forget that in communicating the gospel we may be performing a far greater service for the Kingdom of God if we invite others to give.

This then forms the first step in the "raised question." "What do you have to give to me? Tell me of your beliefs. Tell me what you feel. What do you think? Give me something of your life." No man is so deprived or so lost that he cannot give something of himself to us. It is no secret that any good form of communication must proceed by inviting the one to whom the message is given into the life of the one who is sending it. The church school teacher invites students into his life. The preacher, the pastor, the administrator establishes a rapport which is something more than getting everyone quiet. It is the invitation to focus upon the relationship that is being established. Moreover, it is something more than merely a sort of trickery to get people into a mood to accept what propositions we may have to offer or prepare for the witness we may want eventually to give. To ask another to express his belief, to tell what he feels, to open his life for us, is in itself a form of witnessing. It implies that we become completely attentive, in the ways discussed in an earlier chapter.

As the encounter proceeds, we discover what the relationship itself means to the person or group. It will soon become apparent whether or not we are interested in establishing an environment of free exchange. As another understands our gesture, word, emotional tone, and openness, we will be able to sense what the situation means to him, and first of all we should expect that in many cases it will mean probably nothing. It is surprising how many people are quite satisfied to maintain their communication at superficial levels. It is not that people are uninterested in raising important questions about life; rather, they have so firmly established their forms of communication that any variation from these paths are strange and unwanted. We must accept the fact they want us to function on the levels they understand simply as a reminder that they are a part of the world and they have someone to whom they can go if the need becomes serious enough.

Questions Raised in the Encounter

Suppose, however, these persons are attracted to us by the fact that we have permitted them to give us something. What other questions need to be raised? In what way do we search for the authority of God's Spirit in this relationship? There are three such questions that need to be asked so that they become a part of the encounter. They are the invitation, the bidding gesture, the only authority to which ultimately the Christian can appeal – that where " two or three are gathered in my name, there am I in the midst " (Matt. 18:20).

The first of these questions is, What can this situation help you to mean to yourself? Already in our relationship with the other, by inviting him into our life to give us something of himself, we have already given him sufficient security to be himself in our presence. He may not be interested in what we have said. Even if he is opposed to the faith we represent, he will feel nonetheless secure because we have helped him mean something to himself, because the situation is a cordial one, and within it the understanding of himself and the situation in which he finds himself is such that he can speak and think freely. He feels worth-while and realizes that the situation includes him as well as others around him. The Christian does his " bidding " by assuming an attitude of " high neutrality." This is the art of testing the others level of readiness. It is inevitable that our energy level and spiritual well-being will govern our gestures toward others, and to deny our true feelings will serve no useful purpose in the event. But to the degree that we can postpone gratification of these feelings, we will thus invite the other to establish the mood of the encounter.

At the same time the Christian raises the question as to

what the situation can mean to the other one, he raises the question as to what it can mean for himself. He is not a silent partner, or a spectator, or a presiding officer at the growth of another. He is within the growth pattern. He reflects, responds, returns, but not without constant reference to himself. When we try to give understanding to others, we do not lose our own need for understanding and acceptance. It is this self-involvement which keeps our neutrality from reaching absurd proportions. Even when Christians meet Christians, they are instructed to "wait on one another." No matter how closely related we may be, the initial moments in any encounter may make the difference between the establishment of an authority from within one of the participants or "bidding" the coming of the authority of God among them.

The second question is equally important and should be raised only after the first question has been answered to an acceptable degree. It is, What can we mean to each other? Once we get past the situation itself we always come to the individuals in it. When we enter a stadium, we are first attracted by the mob and the vastness of the scene, but as we become accustomed to it we begin to notice the people around us, to isolate faces from the crowd, and to focus on events close to us. In normal relationships we move from the general to the specific. Upon feeling comfortable within a situation we will be relaxed enough to focus upon the person, but until we feel this sort of comfort we look for ways of escape or a polite way to dissociate ourselves from the discomfort. If the situation remains comfortable, we are able then to let our eyes roam away from possible exits and fix upon the one who is there.

It is impossible to expect the Christian encounter to gain authoritative insight until something has happened to draw the participants into meaningful interaction. Faith in this basic human event must be reiterated to the Christian community again and again. If Christians were deprived of all the mechanisms of communication and separated from all our curricular niceties, and if we were forced to give up all the accouterments of our vast educational program, we would still be left with the most important datum for communicating the gospel — the simple involvement of one person with another in matters of the spirit. With all the wealth of resources available to him, the Christian as witness must ultimately rely upon his ability to engage the immature in a search for the authoritative word by which they both shall grow. Within such a situation there is free confession, not only to one's inadequacy as a person but also to the doubts and uncertainties one faces in his quest for authority in this world of relative values. This might look like a long stone's throw from the kind of authority Christians usually employ when the Christian proclaims the word to another, but to ask what the relationship can mean to us is to bid for the kind of circumstances that invite the awakening Spirit of God. When the Christian defers his "personal authority" to the authority God gives, it is possible to accelerate the movement of information and understanding in the event.

As the trust deepens, the more likely it is that we shall listen, participate, share, and understand. It is here that our own beliefs begin to be expressed, *but as our own beliefs.* The other person will understand them as ours and in no way suspect that they should become his just because they are ours. Being Christian, we may assume we have reached a more mature spiritual level than the nonbelief we encounter. But to refrain from such judgment moves the relationship across a crucial point. It is not ours to judge. It is not ours to say, "My belief is better than your belief," or, "Your belief might hold you up under certain circumstances but in others it will fail you." Judgment again belongs to the authority resident in the situation. It is God's Spirit that judges and not the people who possess beliefs about him.

When people open themselves to one another, it is God's Spirit that somehow moves among them with a sufficient judgment, if given time, to sensitize people to what is good and true. Otherwise the situation becomes argumentative and people do not actually seek what each can mean to the other but actually seek ways they can reinforce what they mean to themselves. "As for the man who is weak in faith, welcome him, but not for disputes over opinions." (Rom. 14:1.) If a Christian is to mean something to another person and permit the other person to mean something to him, judgment must not be assumed by the person or the group beyond what the situation can tolerate and work with. When we speak about our belief, it does not sound like something irretrievable. It is regarded frankly as the point to which we have been led, and we are able to state it without judgment.

The third question in the encounter by the bidding spirit is, What is the ultimate meaning of things? Probably more than we suppose, normal conversation gets around to dealing with ultimates. It is hardly conceivable that we should terminate even the most casual conversation without bringing to bear some ultimate enjoinder such as, "Well, everything will turn out all right," or, "This dry spell can't last forever." We do not like to leave things hanging in mid-air. Even in the daily relationships we run into suggestions of ultimate concern. One such is recorded by C. S. Lewis out of his experiences during the Second World War.

> A vet, a workman, and I were wearily stumbling about on a home guard patrol in the small hours. The vet and I got talking about the causes of wars and arrived at the conclusion that we must expect them to recur. "But, but, but," gasped the workman. There was a moment's silence and he broke out, "But then what's the good of the ruddy world going on?" I got a very clear impression of what was happening. For the first time in his life, a really ultimate question was before him. The sort of thing we had been considering all our lives – the meaning of existence – had just broken upon him. It was a wholly new dimension.[54]

Here again it does not take a theologian to raise ultimate questions, even though he makes it his business. It is probably to the discredit of the Christian and the church itself that, in all its educational endeavor, the church has not encouraged people to be "question raisers." It has even been skeptical of the kind of "question-raising" that moves beyond the certainties, let alone raising questions about the certainties themselves.[55]

It seems only reasonable then that in communicating the gospel there should come to the fore questions having to do with ultimate meanings, things of the greatest importance, things we could not do without. The difficulty in accomplishing this end in our relationships is probably only a verification of its importance. Ultimate meanings do not come to the surface easily. They move around rather vaguely in our emotional make-up. We say of them, "Well, it means something to me but I find it hard to express." As Cherry points out, the fact that we are reasoning animals does not keep us from understanding many things for which reason is not employed. Many inventions have come about by "flashes of insight." When someone tells a joke, we laugh without knowing the dynamics of humor.[56] Even the Christian should not be criticized too quickly if he cannot rattle off at a moment's notice the sum and substance of what holds him together and gives meaning to his life. We come into an encounter, then, not with complete adequacy, but with varying degrees of inadequacy. It may be that other persons in the relationship may be far more articulate in expressing their meanings. On the other hand, the Christian may not be too clear or explicit in describing how he feels or what life means to him. This is why it is important to take the next step in the relationship: to invite the question, as though it were the invitation for the other one, regardless of his belief, to help you in your quest toward a stronger belief in what may be quite opposite to the thing he believes.

Here is where the Christian witness reaches its true exploratory character, for it is raising questions to which only the scantiest of answers have been given and for which men have dedicated their lives. Where do I come from? Where am I going? What is the purpose of my life? What is my relationship to God? What ought I do in this world? How can I know the will of God? These questions have eternal relevance. They are not only questions about the eternal, but eternal questions. They do not have answers that flow readily from one person to another. They are the questions that must be solved and resolved within every relationship, and what appears to be successful in one encounter may be completely unsuccessful in another. Even in the most intimate of groups the constant pull and release of these eternal and fundamental questions of life may cause movement in that group to vary.

It is here, moreover, where the greatest faith is needed. To the question, What is the meaning of God and what does God expect of my life? Christians are tempted by ready answers and say, "Yes, we have an answer. Here it is." But only one half this statement is true. We *have* an answer. Without it we have no call to function as convicted persons. But when we say, "Here it is," we immediately open what we have to the judgment of God in exactly the same way we expect the belief of the other to be opened. What we "have" becomes modified "in communication." In a sense, we no longer have it, for it is accomplishing what pleases God. It will return to us in new perspective as new truth.

The authority ultimately rests in what God does among us. It is hard for us to have faith in such a process. So much is left to the unknown. And yet, even the very instant we want to manage these affairs for ourselves we appeal to an authority other than what God does among us. God appears in history at the points where questions of ultimate meaning are raised in human encounter. We are not likely to modify the thought and life of the other to any great degree at any given time, but this is nonetheless the way history moves. For that modification, be it ever so slight, will establish the direction of history in the next moment. Being this crucial, therefore, our statements must have God's meaning. They will maintain a tentative, bidding spirit, ever asking for direction toward the ultimate questions with a view to the knowledge that eventually we shall know whether we are acting within the will of God.

To overcome our loneliness we may "agree to disagree" and discharge our Christian responsibility by repressing the desire to maintain the search when we are found in an encounter with someone whose belief patterns are contradictory to our own. This is the sort of agreement that tacitly suggests that everyone concerned stops growing. The Christian has a constant restlessness about the level and kind of disagreement in the encounter. He is sensitive to the fact that he cannot permit growth toward ultimate meaning and at the same time remain out of tension. He serves two ends: one, to keep alive the relationship; two, to keep alive the tension in which the Christian can bid for God's guidance. It is too easy to serve the interest of the first of these by minimizing or even surrendering the second. The consequence is a permissiveness that surrenders the gospel on the altar of agreement, which is not an end in itself but merely a means to maintaining the tension. And if the Christian accepts the responsibility for raising questions for himself, he will also accept it for others. Within the areas of his relationship with all people, within the church and without it, he will raise the ultimate questions about man's life before God and the meaning of Christ who came to demonstrate the love that characterizes the event in which the questions are raised.

The Art of "Living Among"

It would be absurd to assume that in every single relationship Christians will be able to function efficiently as communicators of the gospel. More often than not, we shall feel frustrated and disappointed. When we are successful, even the success will be only partial or temporary. Communication at the level of Christian meaning is never easy, and only seldom filled with the excitement induced by moments of great insight or experience. If we were to rely only on the infrequent peak points reached in our encounters, we could seriously raise the question as to whether our efforts at witnessing are worthwhile.

Moreover, there is some question as to whether our planned, purposive encounters as communicators accomplish as much as does the simple and natural act as " living among " others. We bring into being countless significant encounters through the unplanned agenda into which we fall as a matter of course. However, " living among " cannot be undisciplined any more than we leave to chance our acts of communication planned especially to engage others in a quest for faith.

First, Christians live with others in confidence that we speak and act " in the name of Jesus Christ." Much time should be spent asking what one needs to say and be *in life* as well as *in the incidents of life.* Mastery of the Christian faith as a supporting content grows out of the constant reflection upon whether for us the " name of Christ " and the " name of Christian " have anything in common. Is it easy for us to turn our thoughts toward God? Do we like the quest for truth? Does the love of Christ provide patience, faith, and concern, even in the midst of trouble? Do we *live* in the name of Christ, as well as speak in " the accents of its tone "?

If these are the Christians' guidings for growth, we shall attract many. We shall be invitational in our bearing, for people will detect in us an inner strength they can draw upon. To be with us, regardless of what is being talked about, or even if nothing is being said at all, will be a source of comfort and assurance. We bring healing and growth by bearing about in our lives a disciplined adherence to the Christian way.

Secondly, Christians are characterized by a movement from " autobiographical " to " mutual " behavior. They act always " as though " others were involved in what they do, whether they actually are or not. Love makes a terrible assault upon our privacy — always figuratively, often literally. Christ makes us permeable, even when alone. With all the current criticism of " togetherness," one can hardly suppose that the answer to the Christian life lies in the other direction. When one functions alone, he can recount only his own deeds and thoughts, and he alone understands his words. If he lives in mutuality, he has a spirit well disposed toward the other; not only a love for persons, but the love for the movement of persons within his own concerns, deliberately sharing with others while at the same time developing self-insight.

On the other hand, only in the broadest sense are our experiences similar. In fact, any similarity of experience occurs at the level of symbol, beneath which is a very private, personal level of feeling. How can one escape being "autobiographical"? Only by understanding that the coming of the gift of love in our lives *is in itself an act of mutuality,* and that every act of the Christian is *communication.* The presence of Christ *is* fellowship, which is carried *among* Christians because it is carried *in* the Christian.

The third characteristic of "living among" is found in our willingness to be an example, or paradigm, of the gospel. The term "paradigm" is stronger than "example." Martin Dibelius uses it to describe the literary form employed by the early church to tell about the revelation of God in Christ. The paradigm was a story, parable, or allegory of the faith that demonstrated its meaning and strength.

Christians are exactly such "parables" of the faith. The declaration of the apostles, "We cannot but speak of what we have seen and heard" (Acts 4:20), is not strange to us. Because of our sin, weakness, doubt, and fear, we shall ever need to communicate by bidding the other one to come with us on a common pilgrimage, but we speak with authority because we are assured that the story of love can be told in every encounter just as it has been told in us.

Notes

1. For a further elaboration of the historical meaning of communication for the Christian faith, see especially F. W. Dillistone, *Christianity and Communication* (Charles Scribner's Sons, 1956); Hendrik Kraemer, *The Communication of the Christian Faith* (The Westminster Press, 1956); and David H. C. Read, *The Communication of the Gospel* (S.C.M. Press, Ltd., London, 1956).

2. Clement of Alexandria, *Christ the Educator,* tr. by Simon P. Wood. Fathers of the Church, Inc., 1954.

3. *Ibid.,* pp. 144–145.

4. Harold J. Grimm (ed.), *Luther's Works,* tr. by W. A. Lambert. Muhlenberg Press, 1957. All quotations from this book are used by permission of the publisher.

5. *Ibid.,* p. 344.

6. *The Religious Telescope* (September 14, 1853), p. 1.

7. Grimm, *op. cit.,* p. 345.

8. W. A. Visser't Hooft (ed.), *The Church's Witness to God's Design* (Harper & Brothers, 1948), p. 119.

9. Grimm, *op. cit.,* p. 355.

10. Dillistone, *op. cit.,* pp. 13–17.

11. See Jurgen Ruesch, and Gregory Bateson, *Communication* (W. W. Norton & Company, Inc., 1951), Chapter 1.

12. *Ibid.,* p. 6.

13. Klaus Von Bismarck, " The Christian Vocabulary: An Obstacle to Communication? " *The Ecumenical Review,* Vol. X (1957), pp. 6–7. Used by permission of the United States Conference for the World Council of Churches, Inc.

14. Ruesch and Bateson, *op. cit.,* pp. 21–22.

15. G. K. Zipf, *Human Behavior and the Principle of Least Effort.* Addison-Wesley, Cambridge, 1949.

16. See especially Matt. 23:13–15, 23–24.

17. Clarence Day, *This Simian World.* Alfred A. Knopf, Inc., 1920.

18. Gardner Murphy, *Personality: A Biosocial Approach* (Harper & Brothers, 1947), p. 47.

19. Joost A. M. Merloo, *Conversation and Communication* (International Universities Press, Inc., 1952), p. 3.

20. *Ibid.*, p. 18.

21. For a more complete description of this difference, see Frieda Fordham, *An Introduction to Jung's Psychology* (Penguin Books, Inc., 1959), Chapter II.

22. An adequate treatment of nonverbal communication is to be found in Jurgen Ruesch and Weldon Kees, *Nonverbal Communication* (University of California Press, 1956).

23. Dorothy Baruch, *One Little Boy.* The Julian Press, Inc., 1952.

24. Gordon W. Allport, "Normative Compatibility in the Light of the Social Sciences," *Religious Education,* Vol. 53 (1958), p. 67.

25. Von Bismarck, *op. cit.*, p. 15.

26. René Spitz, *No and Yes* (International Universities Press, Inc., 1957), Chapter 4.

27. Carl R. Rogers, *Client-centered Therapy.* Houghton Mifflin Company, 1951.

28. *Ibid.*, p. 74.

29. Halford Luccock, in *The Christian Century,* Vol. 72 (1955), p. 360.

30. Harry Stack Sullivan, *Interpersonal Theory of Psychiatry* (W. W. Norton & Company, Inc., 1954), p. 19.

31. Golden Treasury Series, *Essays of Addison* (Macmillan & Co., Ltd., London, 1956), pp. 361–366.

32. Merloo, *op. cit.*, p. 135.

33. See especially Paul E. Johnson, *Christian Love* (Abingdon Press, 1951).

34. Erich Fromm, *The Sane Society.* Rinehart & Company, Inc., 1955.

35. *Ibid.*, pp. 23–24.

36. William E. Hulme, *Counseling and Theology* (Muhlenberg Press, 1956), Chapter 7.

37. Wendell Johnson, *People in Quandaries* (Harper & Brothers, 1946), Chapter 6.

38. K. G. Collier, "Obstacles to Religious Belief," *Hibbert Journal,* Vol. 56 (1957–1958), p. 145.

39. Paul Johnson, *op. cit.,* p. 212.

40. Seward Hiltner, *Preface to Pastoral Theology* (Abingdon Press, 1958), pp. 179–180.

41. Dietrich Bonhoeffer, *Life Together,* tr. by J. W. Doberstein (Harper & Brothers, 1954), pp. 90–91. Used by permission of the publisher.

42. Hiltner, *op. cit.,* pp. 179–182.

43. *Ibid.,* p. 181.

44. Harry DeWire, "Theology and Method," *Religious Education,* Vol. 53 (1958), pp. 429–434.

45. See Howard Grimes, "Augustine on Teaching," *Religious Education,* Vol. 54 (1959), pp. 171–176.

46. Kraemer, *op. cit.,* pp. 12 ff.

47. Von Bismarck, *loc. cit.,* pp. 9–10.

48. Merloo, *op. cit.,* Chapter 4.

49. Ordway Tead, *The Art of Leadership* (McGraw-Hill Book Co., Inc., 1935), p. 108.

50. Ruesch and Bateson, *op. cit.,* pp. 159–160.

51. Kraemer, *op. cit.,* p. 22.

52. Dillistone, *op. cit.,* pp. 98–101.

53. Murphy, *op. cit.,* pp. 161 ff.

54. C. S. Lewis, "Revival or Decay," *Punch,* Vol. 235 (1958), p. 51.

55. For an enlightening discussion of the status of "question-raising" in our educational procedures see Abraham H. Maslow, *Motivation and Personality* (Harper & Brothers, 1954), Chapter II.

56. Colin Cherry, *On Human Communication* (John Wiley & Sons, Inc., 1957), p. 266.

Bibliography

Allan, Tom, *The Face of My Parish.* S.C.M. Press Ltd., London, 1954.

Allport, Gordon W., " Normative Compatibility in the Light of the Social Sciences," *Religious Education,* Vol. 53, 1958, pp. 62–68.

Baruch, Dorothy, *One Little Boy.* The Julian Press, Inc., 1952.

Bonhoeffer, Dietrich, *Life Together,* tr. by J. W. Doberstein. Harper & Brothers, 1954.

Brightman, Edgar S., " Birds in Lime-Twiggs," *Religion in Life,* Vol. 13, 1943–1944, pp. 167–176.

Brown, Roger, *Words and Things.* The Free Press of Glencoe, 1958.

——— Irving Copi, *et al., Language, Thought, and Culture.* University of Michigan Press, 1958.

Buber, Martin, *Between Man and Man.* The Macmillan Company, 1947.

Cantor, Nathaniel, *The Teaching-Learning Process.* The Dryden Press, Inc., 1954.

Chase, Stewart, *The Power of Words.* Harcourt, Brace and Company, Inc., 1954.

Cherry, Colin, *On Human Communication.* John Wiley & Sons, Inc., 1957.

Clement of Alexandria, *Christ the Educator,* tr. by Simon P. Wood. Fathers of the Church, Inc., 1954.

Collier, K. G., "Obstacles to Religious Belief," *Hibbert Journal,* Vol. 56, 1957–1958, pp. 140–147.

Cully, Iris V., *The Dynamics of Christian Education.* The Westminster Press, 1958.

Day, Clarence. *This Simian World.* Alfred A. Knopf, Inc., 1936.

De Forest, Izette, *The Leaven of Love.* Harper & Brothers, 1954.

DeWire, Harry, "Theology and Method," *Religious Education,* Vol. 53, 1958, pp. 429–434.

Dillistone, F. W., *Christianity and Communication.* Charles Scribner's Sons, 1956.

Fordham, Frieda, *An Introduction to Jung's Psychology.* Penguin Books, Inc., 1959.

Fromm, Erich, *The Sane Society.* Rinehart & Company, Inc., 1955.

—— *The Meaning of Love.* Harper & Brothers, 1956.

Grimes, Howard, "Augustine on Teaching," *Religious Education,* Vol. 54, 1959, pp. 171–176.

Grimm, Harold J., ed., *Luther's Works,* tr. by W. A. Lambert. Muhlenberg Press, 1957.

Hall, Edward T., *The Silent Language.* Doubleday & Co., Inc., 1959.

Hamilton, William, *The Christian Man.* The Westminster Press, 1956.

Heider, Fritz, *The Psychology of Interpersonal Relations.* John Wiley & Sons, Inc., 1958.

Highet, Gilbert, *The Art of Teaching.* Alfred A. Knopf, Inc., 1952.

Hiltner, Seward, *Preface to Pastoral Theology.* Abingdon Press, 1958.

—— *The Christian Shepherd.* Abingdon Press, 1959.

Hulme, William E., *Counseling and Theology.* Muhlenberg Press, 1956.

Jespersen, Otto, *Language, Its Nature and Development.* George Allen & Unwin, Ltd., London, 1949.

Johnson, Paul E., *Christian Love.* Abingdon Press, 1951.

Johnson, Wendell, *People in Quandaries.* Harper & Brothers, 1946.

Kraemer, Hendrik, *The Communication of the Christian Faith.* The Westminster Press, 1958.

Maslow, Abraham H., *Motivation and Personality.* Harper & Brothers, 1954.

Merloo, Joost A. M., *Conversation and Communication.* International Universities Press, 1952.

Miller, George A., *Language and Communication.* McGraw-Hill Book Co., Inc., 1951.

Montagu, Ashley, *The Meaning of Love.* The Julian Press, Inc., 1953.

Murphy, Gardner, *Personality: A Biosocial Approach.* Harper & Brothers, 1947.

Murray, John, *The Daily Life of the Christian.* S.C.M. Press, Ltd., London, 1955.

Ogden, C. K., and J. A. Richards, *The Meaning of Meaning.* Harcourt, Brace and Company, Inc., 1956.

Overstreet, Bonaro W., *The Responsibility Is Ours.* Freedom Pamphlets, 1948.

Read, David H. C., *The Communication of the Gospel.* S.C.M. Press, Ltd., London, 1956.

Rogers, Carl R., *Client-centered Therapy.* Houghton Mifflin Company, 1951.

Ruesch, Jurgen, *Disturbed Communication.* W. W. Norton & Company, Inc., 1957.

Ruesch, Jurgen, and Bateson, Gregory, *Communication.* W. W. Norton & Company, Inc., 1951.

——— and Kees, Weldon, *Nonverbal Communication.* University of California Press, 1956.

Slavson, S. R., *Character Education in a Democracy.* Association Press, 1939.

Spitz, René, *No and Yes.* International Universities Press, Inc., 1957.

Stewart, David A., *Preface to Empathy.* Philosophical Library, Inc., 1956.

Sullivan, Harry Stack, *Interpersonal Theory of Psychiatry.* W. W. Norton & Company, Inc., 1953.

Tead, Ordway, *The Art of Leadership.* McGraw-Hill Book Co., Inc., 1935.

Tillich, Paul, "The Word of God," in Ruth Anshen, ed., *Language: An Inquiry to Its Meaning and Function.* Harper & Brothers, 1957.

Tittle, Ernest Fremont, *Christians in an Unchristian Society.* Association Press, 1939.

Von Bismarck, Klaus, "The Christian Vocabulary: An Obstacle to

Communication?" *The Ecumenical Review*, Vol. X, 1957, pp. 1–15.

Whorf, Benjamin Lee, *Language, Thought, and Reality*, ed. by John B. Carroll. John Wiley & Sons, Inc., 1956.

Williams, George H., "The Role of the Laymen in the Ancient Church," *The Ecumenical Review*, Vol. X, 1958, pp. 225–248.

Index

Acceptance, 97 f.
Accepting and rejecting, 67
Addison, Joseph, 84 f.
Affirmation, 66
Allport, Gordon W., 58
Amsterdam Conference, 25
Attentiveness, 67 ff., 72, 134, 159
Authority, 87, 88, 166 ff.; of the church, 110; finality of, 179; in the raised question, 176; in witnessing, 175

Baruch, Dorothy, 54
Bateson, Gregory, 167
Biblical references: Matt. 6:25 ff., p. 159; Matt., ch. 10, p. 15; Matt. 10:19, p. 64; Matt. 10:22, p. 86; Matt., ch. 16, p. 151; Matt. 18:20, p. 177; Matt., ch. 22, p. 86; Matt. 23:13-15, 23-24, p. 41; Matt., ch. 24, p. 86; John, ch. 17, p. 156; Acts 4:20, p. 185; Rom. 14:1, p. 180; Rom. 15:2, p. 138; I Cor. 1:5-7, p. 22; I Cor. 4:1, p. 27; I Cor. 2:13, p. 56; I Cor. 13, p. 93; I Cor. 14:20, p. 152; Gal. 4:3, p. 152; Gal. 5:22-23, p. 23; Eph. 4:14, p. 152
Bidding approach, 173 ff.
Bonhoeffer, Dietrich, 116
Bultmann, Rudolf, 27
Burden-bearing, 139 ff.

Chatter need, 42
Children, 134, 152, 156; bodily behavior of, 65 f.
Christian, the, 68, 71, 72, 74, 78, 80, 81 f., 86, 88; and communication process, 31, 118, 123 ff.; as communicator, 25, 34; first image, 133 ff.; and language, 31 ff.; and language of the world, 32; and meaning, 60; as a person of God, 27; as redemptive, 100; and right to communicate, 22 ff.; second image, 128 ff.; and social distance, 46; as a sounding board, 160; as theologian, 34 ff.; as a witness, 15, 17, 20, 26, 31 ff., 57, 59, 101, 105, 136, 167
Christian fellowship, the, 35, 41, 44, 46, 58, 113, 116 f., 120, 125, 127, 129, 139
Christianity, 14, 63, 67, 71
Church, 42, 74, 76, 89; building and equipment, 119; and denominational growth, 17; and language, 107 ff.; New Testament, 138; re-creation of, 103 f.; and society, 142; as a subculture, 18

Church school, 43, 86
Clement of Alexandria, 15
Clergy, 44, 66, 68, 73, 86, 107, 108, 128, 164; and right to speak, 23; and theological dogma, 18
Closeness, 155
Collier, K. G., 110
Comfort, 40
Communication, 28 ff., 35; basic concepts, 29; and Christian faith, 19; and culture, 20; development of, 30; as a discipline, 74; disturbance of, 38; and feeling, 151 ff.; and human growth, 33; and human needs, 40 ff.; as language of the spirit, 22 f.; and meaning, 58 ff.; as means to an end, 35; and personality dynamics, 51, 124; process, 50; responsibility for, 14 f., 18 f., 26; right to, 19 f., 22 ff.; and service, 109; and silence, 108; skills, 29 f., 54 ff.; and social distance, 45 ff.; techniques of, 169 f.; types of, 38 f.; understanding of, 28; as verbal expression, 67, 79; vocabulary of, 64
Concern, 162
Creeds, 120, 160
Culture, 21, 23
Curiosity, 40 ff.
Customs, 123

Day, Clarence, 42
Dibelius, Martin, 185
Dillistone, F. W., 27, 170
Directness, 173
Discussion, 70
Doctrine, 15, 150
Dogma, 49, 100, 101 f., 146 ff., 152; and human behavior, 150 ff.

Edifying, 137 ff.
Encounter, Christian, 26, 144 ff., 155; as exploration, 170
Evangelical movement, 16
Evangelism, 15, 164
Eye, the, 68

Faith, 159, 163
Fromm, Erich, 95
Functional authority, 167

Gesture, 108, 164
Gospel, the, as acceptance or rejection, 67; communication of, 19; and human behavior, 63; and the meaning of love, 19; negative communication of, 69, 76, 83; teaching of, 73; and the world, 27
Grief, 139 ff.
Group, 94, 132

Hearing, 51, 124
Hiltner, Seward, 115, 122
Hulme, William E., 102
Human event, 90, 92 f., 121
Human relationships, 31

Incarnation, 100
In-groupness, 46
Interdependence, 94, 97
Interparticipation, 97
Invitational behavior, 175 ff.

Jesus, 15, 37, 41, 53, 59, 61, 64, 65, 76, 85, 86, 93, 115, 146, 154, 155, 159, 170, 184
Johnson, Paul, 111
Johnson, Wendell, 107
Judgment, 20

Kingdom of God, 81
Kraemer, Hendrik, 129

Laity, 143 ff.; in church and culture, 24; as "preachers," 34; and theological dogma, 18
Language, 154, 161; of the body, 54, 65 ff.; and the Christian, 22; limitations of, 32; and love, 107; meaning of, 23; negative aspects, 70; nonverbal, preverbal, and subverbal, 53; of the other, 156 ff.; as symbols of meaning, 75 ff.; types of, 55; and use of eyes and ears, 68
Leader, church, 128, 131
Least effort, principle of, 41
Lewis, C. S., 180
Listening, as attentive gesture, 67 ff.; difficulties of, 68; guidelines to, 73 ff.; as invitational, 71 ff.; levels of, 69 ff.
Love, 19, 37, 45, 47, 53, 58, 62, 90 ff., 121, 122, 124, 126 ff., 133, 135, 174, 185; as action, 91; as bearing, 93 ff.; as believing, 97 ff.; and Christian communication, 91 ff.; as enduring, 100 ff.; as giving and receiving, 175 ff.; as hope, 104 ff.; as a human event, 92 ff.; obstacles to, 105 ff.; as ultimate encouragement, 98
Luccock, Halford, 74
Luther, Martin, 16; and Christian responsibility, 26; concept of man, 19; and right of the Christian, 22

Mass media, 16, 158
Mass-mindedness, 16
Meaning, 58 ff., 117, 137, 147, 149, 181
Merloo, Joost A. M., 89
Mood structure, 115, 153
Murphy, Gardner, 42
Mutuality, 185

Negation, 66
Nurture, Christian, 133 ff.

Paul, 65, 93, 152
Pentecost, 118
Permissiveness, 183
Personality, 54, 70, 74; adequacy of, 37; authentication of, 44; as a field, 50, 165; and integrity, 158; and need to express, 42 ff.; and need to witness, 63; and purpose, 142; and self-extension, 20; and simplicity, 55
Preaching, as verbal expression, 67
Proclaiming, 43
Protestantism, 25, 121
Psychology, 20, 25, 49, 56
Pupil, the, 103, 105
Purpose, 164

Quaker movement, 16
Question-asking, 167

Reformation, 16
Regeneration, 76
Responding, 52
Rogers, Carl R., 71, 79
Roman Empire, 16
Ruesch, Jurgen, 38, 167

Self-acceptance, 106
Self-image, 44
Self-interest, 170
Service, 109

Signal, 29, 123
Silence in communication, 108
Sin, 107
Speech, 52, 115, 122, 124, 157; and Christianity, 71; and interpersonal relationships, 64 f.; language of the body, 65; limitations of, 20; obstacle to love, 105 f.; patterns of, 66 f.; purposes of, 83 ff.; and spirit of the Lord, 64; value of, 77 ff.
Spitz, René, 65
Subtle directness, 176
Sullivan, H. S., 80
Sunday morning, 113 ff., 118 ff.
Symbols, 119, 122, 139, 143, 145

Teacher, 43, 44, 48, 102, 107, 108, 127, 128 ff., 135, 153, 164, 176; as authority, 167 ff.
Teaching, 44, 135, 145; evaluating, 73; with eye and ear, 69; readiness for, 69; techniques of, 129; as verbal expression, 67
Tead, Ordway, 162
Telfer, William, 25
Theologian, 39, 61
Theology, 24, 34, 61, 63, 104, 150 f.

Von Bismarck, Klaus, 60

Wesleyan movement, 16
Wholeness, need for, 33
Witnessing, 14, 19, 63, 78, 86; definition, 175
Words, 148 ff., 155
Worker, church, 131
Worship, 25, 44, 115, 128, 138, 139